"In this superbly written and clearly argued little book, Richard Horsley restates his case for a prophetic Jesus actively engaged in the struggle against Roman imperial rule. But this time he brings to the table new claims about method and sharp criticism for both the defenders and opponents of Schweitzer's apocalyptic hypothesis. . . . Scholars and questers of every level of expertise will want to read this new book from one of our most prolific and treasured scholars."

— **Stephen J. Patterson**
Willamette University

"Horsley persuasively argues that neither Jesus' sayings nor apocalyptic texts (Daniel, *1 Enoch*) envision 'cosmic catastrophe' or the 'end of the world.' Rather, in the midst of historical crises, these texts proclaim judgment of oppressive empires and restoration of the people by God — a compelling future on earth."

— **Barbara R. Rossing**
Lutheran School of Theology at Chicago

"This stimulating study offers insightful critique, important challenge, and significant results."

— **Warren Carter**
Brite Divinity School

The Prophet Jesus and the Renewal of Israel

Moving Beyond a Diversionary Debate

———— ∞∞∞ ————

Richard Horsley

WILLIAM B. EERDMANS PUBLISHING COMPANY

GRAND RAPIDS, MICHIGAN / CAMBRIDGE, U.K.

Published 2012 by

Wm. B. Eerdmans Publishing Co.

2140 Oak Industrial Drive N.E., Grand Rapids, Michigan 49505 /

P.O. Box 163, Cambridge CB3 9PU U.K.

Printed in the United States of America

18 17 16 15 14 13 12   7 6 5 4 3 2 1

Library of Congress Cataloging-in-Publication Data

Horsley, Richard A.

The prophet Jesus and the renewal of Israel: moving beyond a diversionary debate /
Richard Horsley.

p.   cm.

Includes bibliographical references and index.

ISBN 978-0-8028-6807-7 (pbk.: alk. paper)

1. Jesus Christ — Historicity.   I. Title.

BT303.2.H57   2012

232.9′08 — dc23

2012022083

www.eerdmans.com

Contents

—∞∞∞—

CONTENTS

Introduction

⁓

This book responds briefly and provisionally to what I see as two major problems in current discussion of the historical Jesus. The first is the debate over the apocalyptic Jesus that has dominated recent scholarly debate about Jesus, particularly in the United States. The second is the focus of most investigations of the historical Jesus on the individual sayings of Jesus as part of the dominant individualism of this subfield in New Testament studies.

The first is the legacy of Albert Schweitzer. By the late nineteenth century liberal theology had established a highly influential view of Jesus as a teacher of individual ethics and piety. For liberals, the kingdom of God was "within" and/or something that would be gradually realized through social progress. The discovery, translation, and examination of more ancient Jewish "apocalyptic" texts, however, gradually came to convince biblical scholars such as Johannes Weiss and Schweitzer that "apocalypticism" was dominant in ancient Judaism. In opposition to liberal theology, moreover, they came to believe that Jesus, along with John the Baptist and the early Christians, shared the supposedly widespread Jewish expectation of an imminent time of tribulation, last judgment, and end of the world. After Schweitzer's influential sketch of "the apocalyptic Jesus," this view of Jesus became dominant for much of the twentieth century. The construction of Jewish apocalypticism that he presupposed, moreover, became consolidated in biblical studies generally, as well as in study of Jesus and the Gospels.

While suspicions about apocalypticism persisted in German theology, the apocalyptic Jesus jumped the Atlantic and became dominant in North American understanding of Jesus. By the late twentieth century, sufficient doubts about Jesus' belief in the end of the world had arisen for critical neo-liberals to construct a non-apocalyptic view of the historical Jesus as a teacher of wisdom. Other scholars responded with a strong defense of Schweitzer's apocalyptic Jesus. The debate continues, with both sides reasserting their respective views. The American debate at the turn of the twenty-first century is reminiscent of the German Protestant debate at the turn of the twentieth century. Just as Schweitzer's apocalyptic Jesus was a reaction to the liberals' Jesus, so the neo-Schweitzerians' revival of the apocalyptic Jesus is reacting to the neo-liberals' non-apocalyptic Jesus.

Significantly, both sides in the American debate over the apocalyptic Jesus continue to assume that apocalypticism was prominent if not dominant in Judaism at the time of Jesus, and that John the Baptist and the early Christians shared in this view. The neo-liberals insist only that Jesus himself and perhaps his first followers somehow cut through the apocalyptic expectation of last judgment and the end of the world.

In the course of the twentieth century, however, biblical studies became an increasingly diverse — one might even say splintered — field, with many subfields and "criticisms." Specialists in one subfield worked independently of those in another subfield. The burgeoning quantity and complexity of scholarship made it difficult for specialists in particular areas to keep up with developments in the others. Of special potential import for debates about the historical Jesus are recent studies of late second-temple Judean texts. The last generation of scholarly specialists have developed a more complex and precise understanding of apocalyptic texts than the portrayal of "apocalypticism" presupposed by Schweitzer and Bultmann that, with some variations, is still standard in New Testament studies. This raises the question of whether the neo-liberals and the neo-Schweitzerians might be debating more about a century-old scholarly construct of "apocalypticism" than about different expectations or attitudes attested in the ancient texts.

The second major problem, the focus on individual sayings that has become standard in investigation of the historical Jesus, is illustrated by both the neo-liberal studies and the neo-Schweitzerian presentations. This narrow focus is problematic for a number of reasons. Focus on individual sayings (purposely) isolated from their literary context in the Gospels relinquishes one of the only possible guides to their ancient meaning-context. Into the vacuum come various theological schemes to provide a meaning-context and, in effect, to determine the meaning and/or application. Focus on isolated individual sayings thus makes them easily manipulable as "prooftexts" for particular concepts or points.

Focus on individual sayings also tends to reify them as statements or principles or precious nuggets of wisdom abstracted from the contingencies of historical life. Tellingly, standard study of the historical Jesus is specially concerned about the transmission of particular sayings, as if they were precious objects being "handed (down)" from one person to another. The resulting picture of Jesus is as a revealer who, unengaged with concrete historical life, utters one-liners. To have become a historically significant figure, Jesus must have communicated with people, particularly his followers. But it is difficult to imagine that anyone could communicate merely in individual sayings.

In taking individual sayings as the sources or the "data" for constructing the historical Jesus, standard studies are treating the Gospels as mere collections of individual sayings and small individual stories of various types. In the last generation, however, specialists studying the Gospels are insisting that they are sustained narratives, whole stories about Jesus and his mission, and not mere collections of Jesus-traditions. The standard focus on individual sayings, working with an understanding of the Gospels from over a generation ago, may be ignoring the literary integrity of the Gospels as the principal sources for the historical Jesus.

The methodological individualism of the focus on individual sayings, however, is only one key facet of the general individualism of standard study of Jesus as it is embedded in the wider modern western culture of individualism. This individualism, moreover, is compounded by the modern western separation of religion from political-economic life. The individual is the locus, the last bastion, as it were, of religion. In academic study as well as in the society generally, Jesus, the Gospels, and the New Testament are categorized as religious. The study of Jesus is carried out by biblical scholars, trained in a branch of theological studies and teaching in religion or theology departments. The ancient world in which Jesus worked, however, did not separate religion from political-economic life in this way. And the Gospel sources for Jesus present him as fully engaged in the political-economic-religious life and forms of his society. Thus standard study of Jesus may be presenting a reductionist picture of the historical figure, domesticated for people of modern individualist culture.

The presentation below will come in two major steps. Part One will critically examine the recent debate between American scholars over the apocalyptic Jesus, and Part Two will sketch a provisional response and alternative to the prevailing individualism of Jesus studies. Since both liberal and neo-Schweitzerian studies of Jesus exemplify the focus on individual sayings, the examination in Part One will set up the exploration in Part Two. Some of us engaged in historical investigation of Jesus' mission have serious doubts about the validity of focusing on individual sayings of Jesus as historical method. But it is important and only appropriate to probe the debate over the apocalyptic Jesus on its own terms, to check whether the sayings cited by the two sides in the debate actually attest what they claim, and then to check whether the construction of Jewish apocalypticism they presuppose is attested in Judean apocalyptic texts.

The first question, about the recent debate over the apocalyptic Jesus, can be explored in four steps. First, to understand where the debate is coming from, we review the apocalyptic scenario that Jesus supposedly preached and acted out, according to Schweitzer and Bultmann. Second, we review the neo-liberal construction of a non-apocalyptic (sapiential) Jesus (with the apocalyptic John the Baptist as foil) and examine the sayings adduced to attest their portrayal. Third, we review the neo-Schweitzerians' reassertion of the apocalyptic Jesus and examine whether the sayings of Jesus adduced attest the claim that he preached the apocalyptic scenario. Fourth, we examine whether Judean apocalyptic texts attest the apocalyptic scenario that both the neo-liberal and neo-Schweitzerian Jesus scholars assume and in terms of which they are debating about whether Jesus was apocalyptic. Chapter 5 then poses critical questions about the older construct of apocalypticism that has been so influential in Jesus studies, and presents an alternative reading of apocalyptic texts and questions about how they can be used as historical sources.

The chapters of Part Two then present a provisional exploration of a much broader alternative approach than the focus on individual sayings. Pursuit of this broader relational and contextual approach, which takes the Gospels as the historical sources, results in an alternative picture of Jesus as a prophet leading a movement. This exploration also develops in four steps. Chapter 6 presents a brief critique of the narrow focus on individual sayings and then a sketch of an approach that, taking the Gospels as whole texts, attempts to understand the historical Jesus in interaction with people in the crisis of his historical context in Roman Galilee and Judea. Chapter 7 explores the historical context in which Jesus worked, focusing particularly on the many movements of resistance and renewal, both among scribal circles and among the ordinary people, in which the forms and leadership of the movements were informed by Israelite tradition. Chapter 8 is devoted to how we might appropriately understand especially the earliest Gospel texts, Mark's story and the series of speeches paralleled in Matthew and Luke, as sources for the historical Jesus. Chapters 9 and 10, finally, attempt to use mainly those earliest Gospel sources in pursuing the relational and contextual approach to the historical Jesus in historical context. The result is a picture of Jesus as a prophet generating a movement of renewal of Israel over against the rulers of Israel.

PART I

The Apocalyptic Jesus: A Diversionary Debate

CHAPTER ONE

The Apocalyptic Scenario in Schweitzer and Bultmann

———∽∾∾∾———

Albert Schweitzer's and Rudolf Bultmann's sketch of "the apocalyptic scenario" of Judaism that they believe Jesus shared shaped how Jesus was understood through much of the last century. A summary of their sketch will provide some perspective on what neo-liberals are reacting against in their construction of an alternative, "sapiential" Jesus and a sense of the apocalyptic Jesus that the neo-Schweitzerians are restating. Not all of the features that one or both sides of the debate consider apocalyptic are key events or themes in the scenario. But most of them depend on this end-of-the-world scheme that twentieth-century scholars came to believe was prominent in "Judaism" at the time of Jesus.

In his own construction of the historical Jesus (summarized at the end of *Quest of the Historical Jesus*,[1] to which the following makes reference), Schweitzer insisted that not just the preaching of Jesus but his whole public work had to be understood in terms of the apocalypticism that (he believed) pervaded Jewish expectation at the time (QHJ 350-97). In his distinctively theological formulation, "eschatology is simply 'dog-

---

1. Albert Schweitzer, *The Quest of the Historical Jesus: A Critical Study of Its Progress from Reimarus to Wrede* (New York: Macmillan, 1961; 1968), pp. 350-97, which is followed here, since many readers will have used it; *The Quest of the Historical Jesus: First Complete Edition* (Minneapolis: Fortress, 2001).

matic history' — history as moulded by theological beliefs — which breaks in upon the natural course of history and abrogates it" (351).

Schweitzer thought that the eschatology of the earliest Christian community was identical with Jewish eschatology. Therefore the eschatology of Jesus could only be interpreted on the basis of the intermittent Jewish apocalyptic literature from the book of Daniel (early second century BCE) to the book of 4 Ezra (early second century CE). Historically, John the Baptist, Jesus, and Paul "are simply the culminating manifestations of Jewish apocalyptic thought" (367). "We are, therefore, justified in first reconstructing the Jewish apocalyptic of the time independently out of [Matthew, Mark, and Paul], . . . in bringing the details of the discourses of Jesus into an eschatological system. . . ." After Schweitzer, it became standard for interpreters to understand Jesus' sayings according to an eschatological system, an "apocalyptic scenario" that was derived eclectically from Jewish apocalyptic literature. And it is not difficult to discern the influence of passages from Matthew, Mark, and even Paul in the set of "events" or "themes" that comprise "the apocalyptic scenario" that, since Schweitzer, Jesus has been understood to have preached.

For Schweitzer, Jesus' preaching of the coming of the Kingdom of God signaled the end of history, end of the world. For his Jesus, the Kingdom was symbolically and even temporally connected with the harvest (and harvest imagery has since been read as symbolic of apocalyptic judgment and/or consummation). Jesus' statement to the disciples that they would not have gone through all the towns of Israel "before the Son of Man comes" in Matthew 10:23 was the key. Assuming that Jesus viewed himself as the coming Son of Man, Schweitzer identified the Son of Man's coming with the *Parousia* spoken of by Paul and Matthew 25. Taking Matthew 10:23 literally, Schweitzer claimed that Jesus believed that "the Parousia of the Son of Man, which is logically and temporally identical with the dawn of the Kingdom, will take place before [the disciples sent out to gather in the 'harvest'] shall have completed a hasty journey through the cities of Israel to announce it" (358-59).

Indeed, Schweitzer took the whole mission discourse in Matthew 10 as a prediction of the events of the "time of the end," which was immediately at hand. In the predicted course of eschatological events, the Parousia of the Son of Man was "to be preceded by a time of strife and confusion — as it were, the birth-throes of the Messiah" (362). This is the general eschatological time of tribulation to which the closing petition in the Lord's Prayer refers (the "testing"). Another integral event in the apocalyptic scenario was the resurrection, the eschatological metamorphosis of people into a transformed condition. Schweitzer viewed the resurrection and the Parousia of the Son of Man as simultaneous, as "one and the same act" (366).

Schweitzer insisted that this grand apocalyptic scenario was utterly independent of any "national movement" or current historical events or even a general eschatological movement. John the Baptist and Jesus themselves "set the times in motion." By their call to "repent, for the Kingdom of Heaven is at hand," they created a "wave of apocalyptic enthusiasm" (370). And in his own distinctive contribution to the "quest of the historical Jesus," Schweitzer believed that because the final tribulation, the cataclysm of the coming of the Kingdom, and the Parousia of the Son of Man did not happen as he had predicted in Matthew 10:23, Jesus attempted to force the eschatological events (389-90). Jesus then attempted to compel the coming of the Kingdom by violently cleansing the Temple and provoking the Pharisees and the rulers to kill him.

Bultmann similarly declared that Jesus' message of the Kingdom of God "stands *in the historical context of Jewish expectations about the end of the world and God's new future*."[2] His message is not determined by the national hope of the restoration of the kingdom of David by the royal Messiah or of the gathering of the twelve tribes. It is rather related to the hope of other circles documented by "the *apocalyptic* literature." Apocalyptic expectations look not for a change in historical (social-political) circumstances, but a "cosmic catastrophe which will do away with all conditions of the present world as it is." According to Bultmann's summary, the apocalyptic scenario includes the same set of events as in Schweitzer's sketch of Jesus. The new aeon will dawn with "terror and tribulation." The old aeon will end with God's "judgment of the world to be held at the determined time by [God] or his representative the Son of

---

2. This paragraph is a summary of Bultmann, *Theology of the New Testament* (New York: Scribner's, 1951), pp. 34-35, with quotations from those pages.

Man, who will come on the clouds of heaven." Thereafter "the dead will arise" and receive their reward which, for the faithful/good deeds will be "the glory of paradise."

Although Bultmann does not lay out details, he understands Jesus' message of the Kingdom of God in the context of this apocalyptic scenario.[3] Time has run out on the old aeon under the sway of Satan; "the Kingdom of God is at hand" (Mark 1:15). "The Son of Man" is coming as judge and savior (Mark 8:38; Matt. 24:27 par., 37 par., 44 par.; Luke 12:8-9; 17:30). Judgment and resurrection of the dead are coming (Luke 11:31-32 par.; Mark 12:18-27). Details are irrelevant given his certainty that the end is at hand, the Kingdom of God is breaking in (Luke 10:23-24; 6:20-21). While not the calculations typical of apocalyptic ("Lo here or there"), since the Kingdom is already "in your midst" (Luke 17:21-22), there are *signs of the time* (Luke 12:54-56; Mark 13:28-29), especially in Jesus' deeds and message (Matt. 11:5 par.). Bultmann's own particular twist lies in his stress on the imminence of the events of the apocalyptic scenario and hence the urgent need for decision on the part of those who heard Jesus' message of the impending cosmic catastrophe.

It must be immediately striking to anyone familiar with the Gospel representations of Jesus that the logic of Schweitzer's and Bultmann's apocalyptic Jesus makes the rest of his teachings — about common social-economic life, subsistence living, and response to persecution, as well as his healings and exorcisms, his debates with the Pharisees, and his pronouncements about the high priests and Temple — more or less irrelevant. For Schweitzer, since the world was coming to an end imminently, any other teachings of Jesus were merely "interim ethics." Bultmann's view was somewhat less logical and more complex. God's demand to individuals, in the face of the impending cosmic catastrophe, was personal decision — to abandon home and family and literally follow Jesus in his travels. Bultmann insisted, however, that this did not mean asceticism, but "an otherworldliness" of readiness to respond to God's summons to "abandon all earthly ties," to turn away from self, and

3. This paragraph summarizes *Theology of the New Testament*, pp. 35-37. Bultmann's sketch of the apocalyptic Jesus is similar, with the same references to Jesus' sayings, in *Primitive Christianity and Its Contemporary Setting* (New York: Meridian, 1956), pp. 83, 87-88.

place oneself at the disposal of others.[4] Bultmann also viewed Jesus' focus on God's call to radical obedience as an attack against *legalistic ritualism,* against all the cultic and ritual regulations of Judaism.[5] Some of my students over the years have commented that, with this conviction that the historical world was coming to a catastrophic End, Schweitzer's and Bultmann's apocalyptic Jesus could not possibly have been "the historical Jesus," but seems like an "anti-historical" Jesus.

Schweitzer's and Bultmann's presentations of the apocalyptic Jesus are also significant as key steps in the approach that became standard in the study of the historical Jesus in the twentieth century: the focus on separate individual sayings of Jesus and citation of them as attestations of the scholarly interpreters' argument and claims. One of Schweitzer's repeated observations in his review of nineteenth-century books on Jesus was that reading the life of Jesus off the pages of the Gospels was utterly unacceptable as historical method. Critical analysis of the texts of the Gospels was a necessary preliminary step. Scholarly attention had been moving ever more narrowly to text-fragments in the Gospels with the increasing awareness of how particular Gospels had their own distinctive perspective and theology. Post-Enlightenment rationalism and naturalism, moreover, had made historians skittish about using the narratives of Jesus' infancy and healings and exorcisms, replete with "supernatural" features, as sources for information about Jesus. The only reliable material in the Gospels was the teaching of Jesus, and scholars were accustomed to reading the teaching in individual verses, separate individual sayings.

As can be seen in their presentations of Jesus, both Schweitzer and Bultmann proceed from the Jewish apocalyptic scheme or scenario that they believe was shared by Jesus, along with John the Baptist, Paul, and other early Christians, and then find and cite or refer to individual sayings of Jesus as illustrations or attestations of particular events or features of the scenario. Schweitzer believed that Jesus' saying in Matthew 10:23b (the disciples he was sending out would "not have gone through all the towns of Israel before the Son of Man comes") was the key for his

---

4. *Primitive Christianity,* pp. 391-92.
5. *Theology of the New Testament,* pp. 313, 17.

whole construction of Jesus' mission, as noted above. He then took other sayings from the preceding mission discourse, with the image of "the harvest" from 9:37, "sheep in the midst of wolves" from 10:16, and other such "tribulations" from the ensuing verses, as evidence for the overall apocalyptic scenario that Jesus was expecting and acting out. Otherwise, he took sayings from here and there in the different Gospels that (he thinks) fit the portrayal he was constructing.

Bultmann, who had refined form criticism of individual sayings and miracle stories at the outset of his career, was more "disciplined," with more carefully considered criteria by which sayings qualified as reliable evidence for the views of Jesus. In fact he did much to refine the approach to Jesus' teaching that focused on individual sayings. It is evident in his presentation, however, that the overall apocalyptic scenario is the model or pattern into which particular Jesus sayings are fitted. The one saying that he cites for the "eschatological judgment" as imminent, Luke (Q) 11:31-32, for example, does not, either by itself or in literary context, suggest imminence. He cites the kingdom sayings in Mark 1:15 and Luke 6:20-22 and his declaration to his followers that they are seeing what the kings and prophets desired to see (fulfillment?; Luke 10:23-24) as evidence of Jesus' preaching that the End is at hand. But none of those sayings suggest anything about "the End."

Schweitzer's and Bultmann's focus on and appeal to the individual sayings of Jesus taken by themselves out of literary context as attestations of one or another motif, or even of the apocalyptic scenario, thus raise questions about this use of the Gospel sources in relation to the apocalyptic scenario that they believed was pervasive in Judaism at the time of Jesus. As we shall see in the next chapters, however, this approach has become the time-honored standard approach in discussion of the historical Jesus.

CHAPTER TWO

The Non-Apocalyptic Jesus

⊶⊷

O nce scholars became convinced that Jesus shared the apocalypticism they believed dominant in "late Judaism," the apocalyptic
Jesus became dominant for much of the twentieth century. But Enlightenment liberalism had not gone away. Insofar as the end of the world
that he proclaimed did not come, was not the apocalyptic Jesus a de-
luded fanatic?

Bultmann avoided the implication by "demythologizing" the
prescientific universe of Jewish apocalypticism that he believed Jesus
shared. He combined this with an existentialist interpretation of Jesus'
call to repent: to choose one's own authentic existence in the face of the
cosmic catastrophe.[1] That solution seems to have satisfied nearly a
whole generation of liberal Christians at mid-twentieth century.[2]

Scholarly skeptics, however, began to chip away at key aspects of the
apocalyptic scenario and/or at the belief that Jesus supposedly shared it.

---

1. See especially Rudolf Bultmann, "The New Testament and Mythology," in
Kerygma and Myth: A Theological Debate, ed. H. W. Bartsch, trans. Reginald Fuller (Lon-
don: SPCK, 1953); and essays in Rudolf Bultmann, *Existence and Faith* (New York: Meridian, 1960).

2. Only after his works were translated into English following World War II did
Bultmann become prominent as a Gospel interpreter and theologian in the United
States.

It was argued that Jesus did not see himself as "the Son of Man" and/or that "the coming Son of Man" sayings were not "authentic." Closer examination of key passages in key Judean apocalyptic texts suggested that "the son of man" was not a title of an eschatological judge. Other specialists argued that particular "kingdom of God" sayings do not speak of the kingdom as both eschatological and imminent, and some may not be authentic.[3]

Finally toward the end of the century, liberal leaders of the "Jesus Seminar" expressed serious doubts that Jesus himself had proclaimed the imminent end of the world. In his scholarly-autobiographical presentation of "A Temperate Case for a Non-Eschatological Jesus," Marcus Borg[4] stated two key points that knocked the props out from under the apocalyptic Jesus: First, "the coming Son of Man" sayings were virtually the only basis for the modern scholarly sense that Jesus preached the imminent end of the world. Second, Jesus' kingdom of God sayings viewed by themselves, apart from the "coming Son of Man sayings," do not speak of an imminent end of the world, perhaps not of the end of the world at all. Borg and other liberal interpreters, however, still believed that the apocalyptic scenario was prominent in "Judaism" at the time of Jesus, that John the Baptist preached imminent apocalyptic judgment, and that the early Christians shared the apocalyptic perspective, focused on Jesus as the "Lord" or "Son of Man" whose *parousia* (coming) was imminent. Indeed, it was their continuing belief in "apocalyptic" Judaism and the "apocalyptic" expectations of the early Christians that set the framework for their construction of a non-apocalyptic Jesus. They could explain (away) the "apocalyptic" sayings of Jesus as secondary additions to the "sapiential" sayings that they argued were earlier or "authentic." As Robert Funk stated it, somewhat programmatically,

We can understand the intrusion of the standard apocalyptic hope back into his [Jesus'] gospel at the hands of his disciples,

3. Bruce Chilton, *God in Strength: Jesus' Announcement of the Kingdom* (Linz, Austria: Plöchl, 1979), and his "Introduction," in Chilton, ed., *The Kingdom of God in the Teaching of Jesus* (Philadelphia: Fortress, 1984).

4. Marcus Borg, "A Temperate Case for a Non-Eschatological Jesus," *Foundations and Facets Forum* 2, no. 3 (1986): 81-102.

some of whom had formerly been followers of the Baptist: . . . they reverted to the standard, orthodox scenario once Jesus had departed from the scene.[5]

More than any other recent interpreters of Jesus, the liberal leaders of the Jesus Seminar start from and focus on individual sayings of Jesus purposely isolated from their literary context in the Gospels. They believe that this is necessary both because the Gospels impose a distorting "kerygmatic" (early Christian preaching) or theological perspective and because (in their judgment) many of the sayings are secondary. They may disagree with Bultmann's belief that Jesus proclaimed a cosmic catastrophe. But they have developed the form criticism he pioneered into a highly sophisticated investigation of the forms of individual sayings and of the history of the application and interpretation of those sayings in Gospel literature. Through this procedure they sort out the earliest sayings with the best claim to "authenticity" as the "database" for their construction of what Jesus probably said. On this "database" the liberals argue that Jesus was a teacher of wisdom who rejected apocalyptic eschatology. In this connection, liberal scholars have drawn heavily on the Gnostic *Gospel of Thomas,* a collection of sayings and parables of Jesus, and on "Q" (short for the German *Quelle*), the teachings of Jesus paralleled in Matthew and Luke, which is standardly understood as a very early collection of the sayings of Jesus.

The most sophisticated and intricately argued neo-liberal presentation of Jesus as a sage, in contrast to the apocalyptic expectations of Judaism, John the Baptist, and the early Christians, comes from John Dominic Crossan.[6] In fact, he presents a sharpened profile of the apocalyptic scenario insofar as it is dichotomized with "wisdom" from the very first pages of his construction of Jesus.[7] "Apocalyptic" was oriented to-

---

5. Robert W. Funk, *Honest for Jesus: Jesus for a New Millennium* (San Francisco: HarperSanFrancisco, 1996), p. 164. For a clear and more nuanced statement of the case, see also Stephen J. Patterson, "The End of the Apocalypse: Rethinking the Eschatological Jesus," *Theology Today* 52, no. 1 (1995): 29-48.

6. John Dominic Crossan, *The Historical Jesus: The Life of a Mediterranean Jewish Peasant* (San Francisco: HarperCollins, 1991).

7. Crossan, *Historical Jesus,* pp. 228-30.

ward the future, "wisdom" toward the present. The former was vengeful, the latter serene. He later explains that by "apocalyptic" or "apocalyptic eschatology" he means "the darkening scenario of the end of the world. . . . [T]he apocalypticist expected a divine intervention . . . transcendentally obvious . . ."[8] — although in the course of his discussion he does not supply references to any texts that would attest this.

At the beginning of his first chapter on Jesus, Crossan sets up John the Baptist as the apocalyptic foil for his construction of Jesus as a sage. He bases his interpretation of the Baptist on the sayings in Luke/Q 3:16b-17.[9] He notes that it is only because of other representations of John's baptism and sayings and the exchange between John's disciples and Jesus in Luke/Q 7:18-28 that we would think of Jesus as the "coming/stronger one." Accordingly he concludes that "John's message was an announcement of imminent apocalyptic intervention by God" as the "apocalyptic avenger" who was bringing "the fire storm" of eschatological judgment.[10]

But in what way are John's sayings particularly "apocalyptic"? That God, on "the day of the Lord," would be coming in judgment with Spirit and(/or) fire, with deliverance and(/or) punishment, had long been the standard message of *the prophets*, well known, for example, from the book of Joel.[11] This prophetic pronouncement of judgment, moreover,

8. Crossan, *Historical Jesus*, p. 238; similar to the understanding in Schweitzer and Bultmann.

9. Crossan, *Historical Jesus*, p. 230.

10. Crossan, *Historical Jesus*, p. 235.

11. The scribes who produced the texts that we classify as "apocalyptic" understood themselves as the heirs of the prophetic heritage, were familiar with prophetic forms, and at points used them. For an example of an oracle of deliverance and, minimally, of judgment (which has nothing particularly "apocalyptic" about it), see the opening section of the Book of Watchers, *1 Enoch* 1–5. The Epistle of Enoch (*1 Enoch* 92–104) is comprised mostly of a series of prophetic woes on the rulers for their exploitation of the people, and except for the Vision of Weeks at the beginning, lacks features that appear in "apocalyptic" literature. See the discussions in George W. E. Nickelsburg, *1 Enoch 1: A New Translation* (Hermeneia; Minneapolis: Fortress, 2004); and Richard A. Horsley, *Scribes and Visionaries and the Politics of Second Temple Judea* (Louisville: Westminster John Knox, 2007), pp. 166-72; and "Social Relations and Social Conflict in the *Epistle of Enoch*," pp. 100-115 in *For a Later Generation: The Transformation of Tradition in Israel, Early Judaism, and Early Christianity*, ed. Randall Argall et al. (Harrisburg, PA: Trinity Press International, 2000).

was closely linked with accusation of having broken the Mosaic covenant and exhortation to repent and obey. The image of the winnowing fork on the threshing floor, gathering the wheat while burning the chaff, is an extended metaphor that matches the dual roles of divine deliverance and punishment in prophetic tradition. But this image has no particular connotations of the "last/eschatological judgment" in some "apocalyptic" scheme.[12] These sayings of John suggest rather a prophet of renewal of Israel through repentance and renewal of the Mosaic covenant, as symbolized by the rite of baptism in the Jordan.[13]

Crossan then finds in Luke/Q 7:24-26, 27, the contrast between the prophet in the wilderness and the palace-dwelling man in fine raiment and the reference to John as the messenger preparing the way (of Mal. 3:1; cf. Exod. 23:20), "an attempt to maintain faith in John's apocalyptic vision."[14] But again the images and allusions are to a prophet, and indeed a prophetic messenger of the covenant, fitting the baptism John practiced.

As illustrated by the characterization of John's sayings as "apocalyptic," liberal Jesus-interpreters such as Crossan begin by classifying or categorizing individual sayings of Jesus; this has been standard form-critical procedure. Although it is often supposed that such classification is by form, it is often more by content. Thus virtually all sayings that contain the phrase "the son of man" are classified as "Son of Man sayings," and those are further classified by whether they refer to "the son of man" as "suffering" or "coming" in the future. Because "the Son of Man coming in the clouds of heaven," thought of by Schweitzer and others as "the Parousia of the Son of Man," was the central event in "the apocalyptic scenario" constructed a century ago, a great number of "son of man" sayings have been classified as about "the (coming) apocalyptic Son of Man." Crossan and other liberal scholars not only assume this classifica-

---

12. The different metaphor of the threshing of the fruit borne from the evil seed sown in Adam's heart at the end of the age to make way for the good in the new age in the late 4 Ezra 4:28-32 is hardly parallel.

13. Since it appeared the same year as *Historical Jesus,* Crossan would not have known the thorough critical discussion of John as a popular movement-prophet by Robert L. Webb, *John the Baptizer and Prophet: A Sociohistorical Study* (JSNTSup 62; Sheffield: JSOT Press, 1991).

14. Crossan, *Historical Jesus,* pp. 236-37.

tion, but greatly expand the category of "apocalyptic sayings" more generally to include nearly any that might refer to judgment, severe sanctions on behavior, and some that Bultmann had classified as prophetic. Perhaps because "the apocalyptic Son of Man" has been the key to construction of Jesus as an apocalyptic preacher, Crossan devotes more than half of his long first chapter on Jesus to an intricate analysis of the "apocalyptic Son of Man" sayings on the basis of which he insists that none of them go back to Jesus.

The sayings so classified, however, are much more varied in their contents and references than the scholarly classification allows. Many of them, perhaps most, do not attest what Crossan and others claim. He accepts the explanations of scholarly specialists that "(one like a) son of man" was not a title in "apocalyptic" texts prior to and contemporary with the time of Jesus. This appears to be his principal basis for denying that Jesus could have used "Son of Man" in reference to an apocalyptic agent. But the assumption that "the Son of Man" in Jesus' sayings, especially "coming in the clouds," was the "apocalyptic judge" whose coming was decisive in the imminent end of the world scenario persists and still dominates the discussion.

Closer examination of the sayings, however, shows that their images and expressions are more diverse. This can be seen particularly in three different sets of sayings Crossan analyzes, starting with those that refer to "the son of man coming in the clouds." In the prototypical "apocalyptic" vision-and-interpretation in Daniel 7, "one like a son of man" coming in the clouds is not the apocalyptic judge but a symbol of "the people of the holy ones of the Most High" receiving sovereignty, i.e., the restoration of the (Judean) people. Thus, similarly, contrary to Crossan's reading,[15] "the son of man coming in clouds" and "sending out the angels to gather the elect" in Mark 13:26-27 (cf. Didache 16:6-8; 1 Thess. 4:13-18) is not an "apocalyptic judge" but a deliverance or an ingathering of the people of God. This is transcendent agency indeed, but in deliverance, with no judgment and with no implications of the end of the world.[16]

15. Crossan, *Historical Jesus*, pp. 243-46.

16. The standard scholarly generalization that the imagery in Mark 13:24-25, preceding 13:26, refers to the end of the world is rooted in overly literal reading of tradi-

Second, while many take the parallel sayings in Luke/Q 12:8-9 and Mark 8:38 also as references to "the Son of Man" as apocalyptic judge, Crossan sees more clearly that "the son of man" or the "I" (Jesus) or God (indicated in the passive verb) in the various versions of this saying is a "protagonist" in the heavenly court.[17] But how is this an "apocalyptic protagonist" in an "apocalyptic sanction" in the "judgment" that is part of "the eschaton's imminent advent"? It was a standard prophetic tradition that God stood in judgment on people's actions, particularly on their loyalty to God and the covenant, that people would face future judgment in the heavenly court on their action in the present, and that the divine punishment would correspond to the offense (as frequently articulated in the prophets from Amos and Micah to Jeremiah). One suspects that the version in Mark 8:38 that includes the more elaborate portrayal of the coming of "the son of man," followed by the kingdom of God coming with power in Mark 9:1, is what influenced the modern scholarly reading of these sayings as pertaining to "imminent" and "apocalyptic/eschatological" judgment. But "the kingdom of God coming in power" suggests a change in political sovereignty, somewhat like the dominion being given to the people of the holy ones of the Most High in Daniel 7, rather than an imminent end of the world.

Similarly, third, with "the son of man sayings" that Crossan renames "apocalyptic correlatives," i.e., Luke/Q 11:29b-30 and Luke/Q 17:24, 26-29, 30-31 ("the day[s] of the son of man" sayings), it is unclear why they should be read as referring to the end of the world. The form of "correlative" was known in the Septuagint version (Diaspora Greek translation) of prophetic books (Amos 3:12; Isa. 10:10-11), and both those passages and the ones in Q refer to what are analogies drawn from past historical events (or social/agrarian experience) to present or future events. As the preaching of Jonah led the Ninevites to repent, so the preaching of the son of man in the present . . . ; as happened in the days of Noah or Sodom, so it will happen in "the days of the son of man." The devastation of the flood and the destruction of Sodom were severe in the extreme, but his-

---

tional Israelite prophetic language of theophany (as in Isa. 13:9-13), of the appearance of God in judgment on Israel's enemies, that was continued in brief passages in only a few Judean "apocalyptic" texts (such as *Testament of Moses* 10). See further Chapter 4 below.

17. Crossan, *Historical Jesus*, pp. 247-48.

tory continued; it was not the end of the world. These sayings are more appropriately viewed as prophetic or historical correlatives.

In the next chapter (12), focused on some of the "kingdom of God" sayings, Crossan sharpens the dichotomy between "apocalyptic" as future and "sapiential" as present. On the basis of his chronological stratification of the sources[18] and his requirement of multiple attestation, he eliminates from consideration many of the sayings previously ascribed to Jesus. In discussing "the kingdom of God," however, Crossan seems to back away from his earlier assertion that he is using "apocalyptic" with reference to the end of the world by a god of vengeance. He now focuses on "apocalyptic" in a more utopian political sense as the "coming act of transcendent divine power that, having destroyed all evil and pagan empires, would establish a rule of justice and a dominion of holiness in which humanity would dwell forever."[19]

As references to "the apocalyptic kingdom of God" he offers *Psalms of Solomon* 17:3-4, 21, 32; *Testament of Moses* 10:1, 3, 9; and *1 Enoch* 63:1-4. The first, not an apocalyptic text, is one of the rare Judean texts that speak of an "anointed" king, son of David, who will restore Israel in its twelve tribes on its land under the rule of God (i.e., a future *historical* restoration). The second is the concluding prophetic oracle in a text that also focuses on the restoration of Israel, in hyperbolic images of vindication similar to Daniel 12:3 and in allusion to God as the heavenly eagle in Deuteronomy 32:11-13. The third is the only passage where "the Lord of Spirits" is termed "king" in the Similitudes of Enoch (*1 Enoch* 37–71), which focuses throughout on the divine judgment of "the kings and mighty ones," the emperors who have been oppressing God's people. None of these texts speak of "cosmic struggle between good and evil," as it has been characterized in scholarly discussion of apocalypticism.[20]

18. Which Dale C. Allison Jr., *Jesus of Nazareth: Millenarian Prophet* (Minneapolis: Fortress, 1998), pp. 13-20, charges is arbitrary.

19. Crossan, *Historical Jesus*, 287.

20. In his earlier discussion of the Similitudes, pp. 106-7, Crossan slips into this standard characterization. He also attempts to bolster the evidence for apocalypticism at the time of Jesus by reading Josephus' accounts of the Fourth Philosophy and the Sicarii as "activist manifestations of apocalypticism" (112-23). Then, in order to have some manifestation of apocalypticism in the "little tradition" that corresponds to the

Although Crossan has backed away from "apocalyptic eschatology" as the end of the world and moved towards the "apocalyptic kingdom" as the future destruction of "all evil and pagan empires," he still contrasts it sharply with the present "sapiential kingdom." The latter he finds in the mystical meditations of the Hellenistic Jewish cultural elite. He cites some passages from the *Wisdom of Solomon* and the treatises of Philo of Alexandria to illustrate how "the sapiential kingdom" is provided to noble souls in the present by heavenly wisdom. This is a curious move for one who has embraced the distinction between what anthropologists and sociologists distinguish as the "great tradition" of the elite and the "little tradition" of the peasants (note Crossan's subtitle).[21] But Crossan is simply following standard philological procedure in which scholars of Jesus and the Gospels have been trained, to focus on individual sayings and to determine their meaning from the occurrence of terms and phrases in comparative material. Standard procedure in New Testament studies trumps the sociology of knowledge: Crossan can find the isolated phrase "kingdom of God" only in a few mystical texts from the Jewish diaspora elite. And the classification of "Jewish" texts as "apocalyptic" versus "wisdom" trumps geographical as well as cultural distance: he offers no references to sapiential texts from sages in late second-temple Judea.

Crossan never gets around to explaining how Jesus' sayings about the kingdom of God — even the ones about the kingdom being particu-

---

texts of the "great tradition," he portrays the popular prophetic (and even the messianic) movements as apocalyptic (158-67, 292). It is gratifying that Crossan found my analysis and presentation of Judean and Galilean popular movements and scribal protest groups useful through much of Part Two of the book. Part of what my presentation in all those articles and the book that followed pointed out, however (perhaps insufficiently), was that these movements and protests were not manifestations of apocalypticism. In *Jesus and the Spiral of Violence* (Minneapolis: Augsburg Fortress, 1993), ch. 5, moreover, I specifically warned about projecting motivation from apocalyptic texts into these movements and protests or into the historical Jesus. For a presentation of what apocalyptic texts and those scribal resistance groups have in common — as opposition to imperial rule — see my *Revolt of the Scribes: Resistance and Apocalyptic Origins* (Minneapolis: Fortress, 2009).

21. I do want to express appreciation that Crossan agrees with the distinction between the official tradition and the popular tradition that I have been pushing for in many publications since the late 1970s.

larly for children in the *Gospel of Thomas* 22:1-2; 22:3-4; and Mark 10:13-16, which he does discuss — relate to "the sapiential kingdom."[22] Nor does he discuss any of Jesus' kingdom sayings that other scholars conclude refer to the kingdom of God as future. Evidently keying on the parallels in the *Gospel of Thomas* 113, 3:1, and 51, he does present the saying in Luke 17:20-21 as meaning that "the Kingdom is already present." The emphasis in the version of the saying in Luke 17:20-21, that "the kingdom is 'among you,'" however, appears to be on the collective social character of the kingdom more than on the present time.

As he moves from John's "apocalyptic" warning about the vengeful judgment of God to Jesus' "sapiential kingdom," Crossan segues from "Son of Man" to "children" and from ascetic fasting to gluttonous feasting in order to arrive at the egalitarian idealism he sees in Jesus' "open commensality."[23] So, following through on Crossan's interpretation of Jesus from Jewish sapiential texts, we can look at the best-attested Judean sage, Jesus ben Sira, who was closer at least in geographical proximity to Jesus of Nazareth than Alexandrian Jewish mystical philosophers. Jesus Ben Sira, moreover, discusses "open commensality" with sinners! He teaches his disciples about eating at table with the wealthy and powerful aristocrats who, he teaches in other sapiential sayings, are exploiting the poor in violation of the Mosaic covenant (Sirach 13:1-13; 31:12–32:13; cf. 13:15-20). He also teaches his disciples to come to the aid of the destitute and to defend them (Sirach 3:30–4:10; 29:8-13). But this typical Jewish sage sees the poor as several cuts below his own status and honor (38:24-34) — and he would never sit down to eat with artisans, much less with peasants.[24] Evidently it would be difficult to get very far explaining the meaning of Jesus' sayings from sapiential texts.

In sum, Crossan argues that Jesus was not apocalyptic by setting

22. In the Wisdom of Solomon and especially in Philo's treatises, children/babes are capable of only elementary instruction and incapable of receiving/attaining wisdom; only the "mature" or "perfect" can attain the serenity of immortality that comes with intimate knowledge of wisdom. See the discussion of Philo texts in Richard A. Horsley, *Wisdom and Spiritual Transcendence at Corinth* (Eugene, OR: Cascade Books, 2008), pp. 12-16.

23. Crossan, *Historical Jesus*, pp. 255-64.

24. See further Horsley, *Scribes and Visionaries*, pp. 133-42.

John the Baptist up as a foil and by denying that "the apocalyptic Son of Man" sayings were from Jesus himself. The Baptist's sayings that he cites as evidence, however, attest not an apocalyptic judgment of a vengeful God, but prophetic declarations of God coming in judgment and deliverance as sanctions on the covenant renewal of the people of Israel. The sayings classified as "Son of Man sayings" turn out to be varied, and it is unclear that any of them are about "the son of man" as an apocalyptic agent of eschatological judgment. In these sayings "the son of man" is rather an image or agent of deliverance or ingathering of the people. Crossan never gets around to explaining how the Jesus sayings that he classifies as "sapiential" are about a "sapiential kingdom." And he offers no confirming comparisons from Judean sapiential texts to help explain how Jesus was "a Jewish sage."

CHAPTER THREE

Reassertion of the Apocalyptic Jesus

In response to liberals' construction of Jesus as a serene sage, other interpreters reasserted the apocalyptic Jesus. They stopped short of repeating Schweitzer's claim that Jesus carried out his public actions as an implementation of apocalyptic expectations. But they claimed that Jesus' sayings indicate that he was proclaiming key events in the same apocalyptic scenario that Schweitzer and Bultmann had discerned in his statements. In a presentation intended for a wide audience, Bart Ehrman basically reverted to Schweitzer's century-old picture of Jesus as a "Jewish apocalypticist." He was convinced that history was coming to an end, that God was about to intervene in "a cosmic act of judgment, destroy huge masses of humanity, and abolish existing human political and religious institutions. . . . Jesus expected this cataclysmic end of history could come in his own generation."[1] Dale Allison offered a more careful restatement of the apocalyptic Jesus.[2] While Ehrman either ignored or dismissed much of

---

1. Bart Ehrman, *Jesus: Apocalyptic Prophet of the New Millennium* (New York: Oxford, 1999), pp. 17-19.

2. In two closely parallel publications: Dale C. Allison Jr., *Jesus of Nazareth: Millenarian Prophet* (Minneapolis: Fortress, 1998); "The Eschatology of Jesus," pp. 267-302 in *The Encyclopedia of Apocalypticism*, vol. 1: *The Origins of Apocalypticism in Judaism and Christianity*, ed. John J. Collins (New York: Continuum, 2008). Allison repeated his case again at length in a 133-page chapter in *Constructing Jesus: Memory, Imagination, and History* (Grand Rapids:

the recent critical scholarship, Allison engaged the liberals in debate, with responses to their approach and to their reading of Jesus' sayings.

Allison is concerned to produce a sufficient quantity of "witnesses" and "truth," by which he means individual sayings of Jesus, to establish a convincing "case" about Jesus. Yet he is skeptical about whether continuing debate among scholars using the standard criteria for the "authenticity" of Jesus' sayings (consistency, double dissimilarity, embarrassment) will result in anything more than further disagreement. Since there is no way to avoid uncertainty and subjectivity, he declares that "the best research program" would be first to choose a "paradigm" or "explanatory model . . . by which to order our data," and only then evaluate the historicity of individual sayings in the Jesus tradition.[3]

Without explaining why — other than that "many [scholars] remain confident that the eschatological Jesus must be the historical Jesus" — Allison declares that this means "we are back with the conventional paradigm of Jesus as eschatological prophet" that derives from Weiss and Schweitzer a century ago.[4] In defending the case for the apocalyptic Jesus he thus also reaffirms the assumptions on which it was based. He insists that Jesus and his associates shared an eschatological vision that permeated their thoughts and energized their activities. Like the Baptist before him and the early Christians after him, Jesus shared the "apocalyptic scenario" of "eschatological expectations" of contemporary Judaism.[5] Thus, while it is not possible to reconstruct "an apocalypse according to Jesus," there is little need to spell out the minutiae of his "eschatological scenario" since "he shared so much with so many of his contemporaries."[6] Indeed, Jesus understood himself "to be in the middle of the unfolding of the eschatological scenario."[7]

Baker, 2010). Insofar as the references to a wide range of supposed parallels from various religions and movements around the world tend to weaken rather than strengthen his case that Jesus shared the apocalyptic scenario distinctive to ancient Judaism, I will focus on the two 1998 statements of his case for the apocalyptic Jesus.

3. Allison, *Jesus of Nazareth*, pp. 35-39.

4. Allison, *Jesus of Nazareth*, pp. 34, 39.

5. Allison, *Jesus of Nazareth*, p. 130; "Eschatology of Jesus," pp. 275-80.

6. Allison, *Jesus of Nazareth*, pp. 130-31.

7. Allison, "Eschatology of Jesus," p. 275.

In presenting his case, Allison focuses on four key "themes" in that scenario and offers sets of Jesus' sayings from the Gospels as illustrations of each one. It might seem that he drops the *parousia* (of the Son of Man), which was the key for Schweitzer. But he adds a discussion of "imminence," for which the principal sayings adduced are the "coming Son of Man" sayings. He also adds "the restoration of Israel," which had no place in the apocalyptic scenario as presented by Schweitzer and Bultmann, but has come to the fore in more recent interpretations of the historical Jesus. We review the "themes" of the scenario, looking in particular for whether or to what extent the Jesus sayings he cites as evidence actually attest them.

"The Eschatological Judgment"

Stating that "the theme of eschatological reversal runs throughout the sayings of Jesus," Allison claims that "this theme presupposes that the eschatological judgment is just around the corner."[8] None of the "reversal" sayings he cites, however, even suggest judgment (much less eschatological or final judgment) or imminence. The blessing of the hungry in Luke/Q 6:21, like the other "beatitudes," refers to God's present-future deliverance, somewhat similar to the reversals in the Song of Hannah and the Song of Mary (1 Sam. 2:4-5; Luke 1:52-53). The "reversals" of "humbled/exalted" in Luke 14:11 and "losing/keeping life" in 17:33[9] are proverbial sayings that depend on their application in Luke and Matthew, respectively, and only in Luke 17:23-37 is the context about judgment (its suddenness). The saying about "first/last" in Mark 10:31 is also a proverb that does not in itself pertain to judgment. In its context it is a sanction on a longer discussion of social-economic criteria of the renewal of Israel ("in this age . . . with persecutions," hence not eschatological) symbolized by "entering the kingdom of God" (Mark 10:17-31).[10]

8. Allison, "Eschatology of Jesus," pp. 281-82; *Jesus of Nazareth*, 131-34; cf. Ehrman's discussion of the same sayings about "reversal of fortunes" in *Jesus*, pp. 148-54.

9. The saying in Luke 17:33 may have been in Q, but Matthew 10:37-39 (and not Luke 17:23-37) represents its "literary context" in Q.

10. The two brief sets of lines that Allison ("Eschatology of Jesus," pp. 281-82) cites

It is a bit of a stretch to claim that the simple warning about not judging one another in a local community in Luke/Q 6:37 "plainly" refers to God's (eschatological) judgment.[11] Two other sayings Allison cites from Q, "that day" in Luke 10:12 and "the judgment" in Luke 11:31-32, do indeed refer to judgment, although neither eschatological nor imminent, but simply a vague reference point in the indefinite future. These and the many other passing references to God's judgment in the teaching of Jesus, however, function as exhortation or consolation or rebuke, as Allison himself points out.[12] Thus the sayings of Jesus that do refer to judgment are not portrayals of "the eschatological judgment" as part of an "apocalyptic scenario."[13]

In contrast to Allison, who does not adduce the "apocalyptic/coming Son of Man" sayings to attest eschatological judgment, Ehrman has no hesitation. While aware of debate about "the son of man" as a title in "apocalyptic texts," he declares boldly that the Son of Man is "the cosmic judge" of the earth coming in destruction,[14] and lists sayings such as Mark 13:26-30 and 14:62 (along with Mark 9:1) as evidence. But none of those sayings refer to Jesus as "the cosmic judge," much less destruction, as discussed in the previous chapter.

Allison admits that there is no passage (including the Matthean representation of the Son of Man giving judgment on the throne, Matt. 25:31-46) in which Jesus spoke of the judgment in any specific way. Yet he insists that Jesus "could take such detail for granted" from familiarity with the Judean apocalypses.[15] Recent research has shown, however, that literacy was limited mainly to scribal circles (i.e., Jesus was probably not literate) and that manuscripts of texts were cumbersome, expensive, and rare.[16]

---

from second-temple Judean texts, Isaiah 60:22 and *Test. of Judah* 25:4, refer not to judgment but to the restoration of Jerusalem/Judea and to the resurrection of martyrs for their loyalty, respectively.

11. Allison, "Eschatology of Jesus," p. 282.

12. *Jesus of Nazareth,* p. 135.

13. Allison, "Eschatology of Jesus," p. 282, admits that these sayings "throughout" the Synoptic tradition do not guarantee that Jesus himself spoke of the judgment.

14. Ehrman, *Jesus,* pp. 144-46.

15. Allison, "Eschatology of Jesus," p. 283.

16. Catherine Hezser, *Jewish Literacy in Roman Palestine* (Tübingen: Mohr Siebeck,

Allison himself seems to be aware that his claim is problematic otherwise as well: "only one text . . . depicts the great postmortem judgment that inaugurates the everlasting kingdom of God." In the one he cites, Daniel 7, however, the giving of the kingdom/dominion to "the one like a son of man," symbolizing "the people of the holy ones of the Most High," refers not to "postmortem judgment" but to a future restoration of the people of Israel — presumably in continuing historical circumstances, hence neither eschatological nor imminent.

In sum, it is difficult to find any sayings of Jesus that refer to God's judgment as eschatological and imminent, as if this were a key part of an "apocalyptic scenario."

"The Resurrection of the Dead"

Jesus also expected a general resurrection, argues Allison. He viewed the eschatological future as some sort of new, supernaturally wrought state to be inaugurated by extraordinary events, including the resurrection of the dead. "In Jesus' teaching, . . . the world after the judgment is . . . the world of eternal life, the deathless life of the angels," which means that "his eschatology is not like that of the old Hebrew prophets but akin to that found in Daniel and later apocalyptic literature."[17] One of Allison's principal bases for this claim is that Jesus was proclaimed as raised from the dead, which he explains from his followers having come to their "Easter" experiences already believing in the general resurrection as imminent, a belief that must have been shared by Jesus himself.[18]

References to (belief in) resurrection in Jesus' teaching are few, however, and involve considerable inference by interpreters. Allison admits, for example, that the exhortation not to "stumble" in Mark 9:43-48, with its extraordinary hyperbole, "makes no explicit reference to the resurrec-

2001); and Richard A. Horsley, *Scribes, Visionaries, and the Politics of Second Temple Judea* (Louisville: Westminster John Knox, 2007), chapters 5-6.

17. Allison, *Jesus of Nazareth*, p. 136; "Eschatology of Jesus," p. 285. The only passage from an "apocalyptic" text prior to the time of Jesus that even briefly refers to the "heavenly" life of resurrection, however, is Daniel 12:2.

18. Allison, "Eschatology of Jesus," pp. 283-84; *Jesus of Nazareth*, p. 138.

tion."[19] On the other hand, Luke/Q 11:31-32 does refer to "the resurrection" as occurring in connection with judgment, in a threatening accusation against "this generation" for not heeding his message. Allison fails to note, however, that the series of speeches that comprise Q evidently know nothing of Jesus' resurrection, suggesting that resurrection was not important in its presentation of Jesus and his teaching. The Gospel of Mark includes the raising of Jesus in its three summaries of the climactic events in Jerusalem (8:31; 9:31; 10:33-34) and has Jesus refute the Sadducees with reference to resurrection (12:18-27).[20] Few critical scholars of the Synoptic tradition, however, would consider these three summaries and the debate with the Sadducees solid sources for Jesus' views. The end of Mark's narrative, moreover, seems to downplay — almost to "historicize" — the resurrection of Jesus himself, focusing on his meeting the disciples in Galilee (14:28; 16:1-8).

In sum, the passing reference to the resurrection in connection with judgment in Luke/Q 11:31-32 is hardly a sufficient basis in Jesus' sayings to project it as a key step in some sort of "apocalyptic scenario" of "eschatological events" that Jesus was proclaiming.

"Restoration of Israel"

For Allison the "eschatological restoration of Israel" focuses narrowly on "the return of the lost tribes" from east and west, etc. Allison is much more critical in his analysis and tentative in his claims about the "restoration" theme than with the other "apocalyptic" themes. Far from appealing to a plethora of passages, not just from the Gospels but from Paul and Acts as well, that might at least indirectly suggest judgment or resurrection, he focuses on only three references. And two of those he acknowledges may be only early Jesus tradition and not from Jesus himself. The "widespread" expectation of the return of the dispersed tribes[21]

---

19. Allison, *Jesus of Nazareth*, p. 140.

20. Allison, "Eschatology of Jesus," p. 284.

21. Allison cites numerous passages from late prophetic, psalmic, and historical texts as well as from post-second-temple "apocalyptic" texts, but few from second-temple apocalyptic texts, for example in *Jesus of Nazareth*, p. 141; "Eschatology of Jesus," p. 300.

Allison finds in the earliest Jesus tradition, specifically in Luke/Q 22:28-30, where the disciples will sit on thrones "ruling" (not "judging") Israel.[22] He is doubtful, however, whether the image goes back to Jesus. Yet it is "surely suggestive," he thinks, that Jesus "associated himself" with twelve disciples. More secure in its attribution to Jesus is Luke/Q 13:28-29, which has traditionally been allegorized into a reference to the Gentiles replacing the Jews in the realization of the kingdom of God. Allison reclaims the prophecy as referring to the future (historical!) ingathering of the dispersed tribes — albeit to replace the rejected Jews of Palestine in the kingdom (which is not obvious in the prophecy).

That Allison's claim for "restoration" as integral to the "apocalyptic scenario" is so limited and tentative should not be surprising. The restoration of Israel was not part of Schweitzer's now century-old tour-de-force. Having come to the fore only recently in the resurgence of interest in "the historical Jesus," it has been inserted into the apocalyptic scenario by neo-Schweitzerians such as Allison. But it stands in acute tension with the other themes as represented in their discussion. The "return" or "ingathering" of the dispersed tribes of Israel to Jerusalem/Judea, that is, the restoration of a supposedly historical Israel on its land, is hardly compatible with "the world of eternal life of the angels" after the eschatological judgment and the "supernaturally wrought" supramundane world of the resurrection of the dead that Allison claims "permeated" Jesus' thoughts and energized his actions. Allison himself feels a tension between the collective (and seemingly "nationalist" and "materialist") restoration of Israel and what he and the neo-liberals alike see as Jesus' "focus on individuals."[23]

---

22. Allison, "Eschatology of Jesus," p. 285; *Jesus of Nazareth,* pp. 141-42, citing Horsley, *Jesus and the Spiral of Violence* (Minneapolis: Augsburg Fortress, 1993), pp. 203-6. I argued, however, that the sense was "delivering" or "doing justice for Israel," as in several Psalms, where God delivers or does justice for the poor, the widow, and/or the orphan.

23. Similarly, Ehrman's interpretation of Jesus' sayings about the kingdom of God meaning that God will at some point begin to rule "here on earth" (p. 142), suggesting that Jesus did not expect the end of history in cataclysm, stands in acute tension with his dominant insistence on the apocalyptic Jesus.

"The Great/Eschatological Tribulation"

Allison asserts that "Jewish apocalypticism is by nature catastrophic." It anticipates a time of terrible tribulation preceding the birth of a transformed world, attested in "the time of anguish such as has never occurred since the nations first came into existence" of Daniel 12:1 and in "the rabbis'" image of "the birth pains of the messiah."[24] He takes "the sorts of disasters catalogued" in Mark 13 as typical of the time of "tribulation." The "beginnings of the birthpangs" in 13:8 seems to anticipate "the rabbis'" image, and the worst suffering since creation in Mark 13:19 is reminiscent of Daniel 12:1. But the references to wars, the suffering they bring for the people, famines, and trials can refer to what were repeated historical experiences of the Judean and Galilean people under Roman rule for more than a century leading up to the great revolt and the Roman devastation in 66-70.[25] The reference to disturbances in the heavenly bodies in Mark 13:24-25 is standard prophetic language in reference to God coming in judgment on and deliverance from foreign (imperial) enemies (see further next chapter). In any case, few critical scholars would attribute the speech in Mark 13 to Jesus himself.

The sayings that Allison cites as evidence that Jesus took up the "traditional motif" of the time of tribulation and used it for his own ends[26] simply do not refer to such a special eschatological period. "Lambs in the midst of wolves" (Luke/Q 10:3) refers rather to the hostile circumstances into which Jesus is sending his envoys in his mission discourse. "The son of man" having no place to lay his head (Luke 9:58) pertains to Jesus' own homelessness during his mission. Those who are poor and hungry and in mourning (Luke/Q 6:20-21) are those to whom Jesus extends the blessings of the kingdom of God. "Hating one's parents" and "taking up a cross" (in Luke/Q 14:26 and Mark 8:34) are hyperbole about the potential costs of following Jesus in the face of persecution. These were the sorts of circumstances that a prophet and his

---

24. Allison, "Eschatology of Jesus," p. 145; but he cites no passages for the statement about the rabbis.

25. See further Richard A. Horsley, *Hearing the Whole Story: The Politics of Plot in Mark's Gospel* (Louisville: Westminster John Knox, 2001), pp. 131-33.

26. Allison, "Eschatology of Jesus," p. 287.

movement would experience in any society such as Roman Galilee and Judea.

In connection with Jesus' presumed self-conception as a prophet, Allison also adduces the Jewish tradition of the persecution of the prophets.[27] That tradition, of course, occurs in historical and prophetic texts, but not in "apocalyptic" texts, and is hardly distinctive to a particular period prior to the supposed supramundane (eschatological) salvation. As indications that Jesus spoke of his own suffering as "belonging to that time" he cites the final petition of the Lord's prayer (Luke/Q 11:4), the reference to divisions among family members (Luke/Q 12:51-53, which in turn alludes to the longstanding prophetic image in Micah 7:6), the reference to fire upon the earth (Luke [Q?] 12:49), and the reference to the kingdom suffering violence since John the Baptist (Luke/Q 16:16).[28] Again upon closer scrutiny, however, Luke/Q 11:4 evidently refers rather to being dragged into court (political repression); Luke/Q 12:51-53 refers to the divisions (even among families) entailed in responses to Jesus' mission, to which his casting fire upon the earth refers in 12:49; and Matthew 11:12-13 refers to the violent repression that prophetic preaching by John and Jesus provoked from the authorities (the saying is isolated in Luke 16:16 and its meaning unclear).[29] In sum, none of these possibly "early" Jesus sayings refer to the supposed eschatological period of "the great tribulation."[30]

"Imminence"

It might seem that Allison has omitted the central component of the "apocalyptic scenario" that Schweitzer believed Jesus proclaimed and

27. Allison, "Eschatology of Jesus," p. 287.

28. Allison, "Eschatology of Jesus," p. 288.

29. At least in the Matthean wording and context of Matthew 11:11-15. In Luke 16:16 the saying is isolated and unclear in its reference.

30. It is unclear how references to "history of religions" books and encyclopedia articles on widely occurring and varied myths and symbols in other cultures, including the cataclysm projected by the ancient Stoics (*Jesus of Nazareth*, p. 145), lend credence to Jesus' having believed in an eschatological period of "tribulation."

was implementing, "the parousia of the Son of Man." Allison is suffi-
ciently attentive to current research on the phrase "the son of man" in
Aramaic texts to know that the coming "Son of Man" is no longer
thought to have been current as the title of an apocalyptic agent of
judgment and/or salvation in late second-temple times. Yet he brings
"future/coming son of man" texts back into Jesus' "apocalyptic scenario" in connection with the theme of "imminence." After presenting
judgment, resurrection, restoration, and tribulation all as imminent as
well as eschatological, he adds a separate discussion to reaffirm that
"eschatological imminence" was "part and parcel" of Jesus' creed.[31] His
discussion focuses on "kingdom of God" sayings as well as "future/
coming son of man" sayings. Without citing any attestation from Jesus
traditions, he states that Jesus expected to see God's kingdom appear
"throughout the whole creation," as in *Testament of Moses* (he probably
has in mind the phrase in 10:1).[32] He lists the references to the kingdom
of God in Luke/Q 10:9 and 11:20 and Mark 1:15 as sayings that ("whatever else [they] may mean") "imply the temporal character of the kingdom."[33] But temporal does not necessarily mean eschatological. And
"the kingdom of God has come upon you" (11:20) indicates already happening, not imminent.

Picking up on a crucial component in Schweitzer's construction,
Allison also appeals to the image of the harvest in both John's and Jesus'
statements as references to the imminence of the eschatological judgment.[34] The harvest in Luke/Q 10:2 and Matthew 9:37-38, however, is not
a reference to judgment but, in the context of the mission discourse, to
the renewal of Israel or to eager crowds. The parable of the sower, Mark
4:2-9, points to the astounding abundance of the harvest despite the dif-

---

31. Allison, *Jesus of Nazareth,* pp. 147-51.

32. Allison, *Jesus of Nazareth,* p. 151.

33. Allison, *Jesus of Nazareth,* p. 148.

34. Allison's lists of prophetic passages in *Jesus of Nazareth,* p. 148 n. 194 and p. 301 n. 15,
however, do not attest threshing as an image of judgment but as an image of military defeat
or conquest. The passages Allison cites to attest that harvest and threshing are images of
eschatological consummation in apocalyptic texts, Revelation 14:14-16; 4 Ezra 4:30, 39; and
2 Baruch 70:2, are all many decades after Jesus, and 2 Baruch 70:1-10 offers an elaborated
list of the "tribulations" of wars, famines, etc., not the consummation.

ficulties, not to its imminence. John's reference to his successor's gathering and winnowing has no temporal reference (Luke/Q 3:17). None of these harvest images suggest something eschatological. Jesus' thanksgiving that God has "revealed these things" to "infants" and not to intellectuals and kings (Luke/Q 10:21) suggests not imminence but events already happening that the people are seeing and hearing, with the emphasis not on the "when" but on the "to whom."

As his "prooftexts" for "imminence," however, Allison relies mainly on Mark 9:1; 13:30; and Matthew 10:23, sayings of similar form "that explicitly make the eschatological kingdom of God temporally near" (148-50). These sayings do speak of either "the kingdom of God" or "all these things" or the coming of "the son of man" as imminent. But nothing in the sayings themselves indicates that these things are eschatological. Only the combination of these sayings with the preceding saying(s) and/or the standard scholarly understanding of "the coming of the Son of Man" suggest that these things are eschatological. If the kingdom of God means, in effect, the renewal of Israel under the direct rule of God, then its coming with power could mean coming (more) completely or fully. What "all these things" are in Mark 13:30 depends on the context, and refers there mainly to "the son of man" coming to implement the deliverance or ingathering of the elect (again, the renewal/restoration of the people). "These things" can be simply future, and are not necessarily eschatological. In any case, for some time there has been a widespread consensus among critical scholars that the discourses in Mark 8:34–9:1 and Mark 13 and Matthew 10 cannot be attributed to Jesus.

In conclusion, examination of the references Allison cites in connection with the main "themes" of the ostensible "apocalyptic scenario" being taught and followed by Jesus indicates that they do not attest those themes — with the notable exception of "the restoration of Israel," which was not part of the scenario articulated by Schweitzer. The sayings of Jesus simply do not provide evidence that he was preaching an "apocalyptic scenario" focused on imminent eschatological tribulation, (leading/prior to) the eschatological judgment, and establishment of a supramundane life of resurrection and eternal life.

Finally, insofar as Allison insists that Jesus shared the eschatological scenario with his Jewish contemporaries, that it was part of the widespread "Jewish folklore" of the first century,[35] we would expect him to cite plenty of references to Judean apocalyptic texts (at least in the notes). Elsewhere in the book of essays on Jesus as a "millenarian prophet" he does cite many apocalyptic and other Judean texts. In his discussion of the themes of the apocalyptic scenario, however, he includes few references to apocalyptic texts, usually bunched with references to prophetic passages and other non-apocalyptic Judean texts, and seldom directly about the particular theme they ostensibly attest.

The debate about "the apocalyptic Jesus" between the leading liberal scholars and the neo-Schweitzerians has continued, even in mutually appreciative direct conversations.[36] Both sides in the debate continue to accept the synthetic picture of apocalypticism — with the exception of the refinement of how "the son of man" is understood — that had become standard at the beginning of the twentieth century. Both Crossan and Allison nudge Jewish apocalypticism into an even broader synthetic cross-cultural scholarly construct of millenarianism.[37] In that connection Crossan cites several standard Jewish apocalyptic text-fragments, and Allison makes a list of millenarian motifs with an eclectic variety of references.[38] But neither the liberals nor the neo-Schweitzerians appear to have looked closely at Judean texts usually classified as "apocalyptic" to determine whether and how they attest the standard "apocalyptic scenario" they both accept as historical. What would happen if we checked the standard picture of apocalypticism against the actual Judean apocalyptic texts?

35. Allison, *Jesus of Nazareth,* p. 131.

36. Dale C. Allison, Marcus J. Borg, John Dominic Crossan, Stephen J. Patterson, *The Apocalyptic Jesus: A Debate,* ed. Robert J. Miller (Santa Rosa, CA: Polebridge, 2001).

37. John Dominic Crossan, *Jesus: A Revolutionary Biography* (New York: HarperOne, 1994), pp. 103-4; Allison, *Jesus of Nazareth,* "Detached Note," pp. 78-94, and 152-69, where he combines references to an eclectic variety of text-fragments (somewhat as Schweitzer did).

38. Crossan, *Jesus,* pp. 106-10; Allison, *Jesus of Nazareth,* pp. 78-94, and 152-69, where he expands the eclectic mix of references of text-fragments from the Jewish and NT texts combined in Schweitzer's synthesis to a much wider mix of cross-cultural references.

CHAPTER FOUR

Apocalyptic Texts, but No Scenario

The surveys in Chapters 2 and 3 show that the sayings of Jesus or John presented by Crossan and Allison as evidence that Jesus did or did not preach the themes of the apocalyptic scenario supposedly prominent in contemporary "Judaism" do not attest those themes. This is not a problem for his argument, suggests Allison, since Jesus could "take such detail for granted" from his familiarity with the Jewish apocalyptic texts.[1] It is striking, however, how little critical attention the scholars engaged in the debate over the apocalyptic Jesus give to ancient Judean texts usually classified as apocalyptic. They seem to assume the standard scholarly view of Jewish apocalypticism. And that appears to have taken shape already by the time of Schweitzer in a set of motifs, themes, and features at the center of which was the basic scenario of apocalyptic events — evidently constructed from motifs and images found in texts ranging from the third century BCE to the second century CE.[2] As

1. Dale Allison, "The Eschatology of Jesus," in *The Encyclopedia of Apocalypticism*, vol. 1: *The Origins of Apocalypticism in Judaism and Christianity*, ed. John J. Collins (New York: Continuum, 1998), p. 283.

2. For an illuminating perspective on the concept of "apocalyptic(ism)" and the lack of continuing investigation into apocalyptic texts after the early twentieth century, see Klaus Koch, *Ratlos vor der Apokalyptik*, translated as *The Rediscovery of Apocalyptic* (SBT 2/22; Naperville, IL: Allenson, 1972).

Schweitzer stated explicitly, moreover, scholars were so convinced that apocalypticism pervaded Judaism and that the Baptist, Jesus, Paul, and other "early Christians" fully shared the pervasive "dogma," that they could use Mark, Matthew, and Paul as sources for the standard scenario of the (supposedly) widely expected cataclysmic end of the world.

Considering that the Jesus sayings surveyed above do not attest the themes of the apocalyptic scenario, the obvious next step would be to inquire critically if Judean apocalyptic texts attest them. That is, given their relative unfamiliarity with Judean apocalyptic texts, can Jesus-scholars "take for granted" the events and themes of the apocalyptic scenario that they believe Jesus (and/or the Baptist) "took for granted"? It would be helpful to know more precisely the views of the circles of Judean scribes who produced the apocalyptic texts.

While there has not been a dramatic change in the basic scholarly understanding of "Jewish apocalypticism" generally since the time of Schweitzer and Bultmann, the last generation of scholarly specialists have developed more critical perspective and greater precision and literary sensitivity in their reading of particular texts.[3] This includes a much less "literal" reading of the texts, and less of an assumption that the texts articulate a worldview or metaphysics. Recent interpreters are less likely to state that verses in these texts are statements of eschatological "dogma," as Schweitzer thought.

Insofar as recent interpreters have sharpened our sensitivity to the literary structure of apocalyptic texts, however, it is no longer possible simply to cite motifs or verses out of literary contexts as "prooftexts" for a given theme in the standard scenario. It is necessary, and only appropriate, to consider literary context, in contrast to the standard way in which these texts were referenced previously. The "visions-and-interpretations" that constitute most of the second-temple apocalyptic texts — Daniel 7; 8; 10–12; the Animal Vision (*1 Enoch* 85–90), and the

---

3. A good example is George Nickelsburg, *1 Enoch 1* (Hermeneia commentary; Minneapolis: Fortress, 2001). More generally, see Nickelsburg, *Jewish Literature from the Bible to the Mishnah,* 2nd ed. (Minneapolis: Fortress, 2005); and John J. Collins, *The Apocalyptic Imagination* (New York: Crossroad, 1983). While these scholars and other specialists will occasionally write of "apocalypticism" generally, they consider particular texts in their historical contexts.

Ten-Week Vision (*1 Enoch* 93:1-10 + 91:11-17) — are short and readily available in good translations.[4] It is easy to read through several to gain a sense of their rehearsals of history, their portrayal of the historical crisis that they address, and the resolution of that crisis in God's judgment and deliverance. (I urge readers to do just this before continuing with this chapter.)

Recent investigations of Judean texts usually classified as "apocalyptic" have also gained a much more precise understanding of the particular historical contexts that they addressed. The history-of-ideas approach has been supplemented and checked by an appreciation of historical circumstances and the political role of the scribes who produced such texts.[5] These recent investigations thus raise questions about whether and how these texts can be used as sources for attitudes and expectations in Judean and Galilean society more generally at the time of Jesus.[6]

Another critical question is whether the late apocalyptic texts, 4 Ezra and 2 Baruch, can be used as sources for the time of Jesus. These texts were composed five or six decades, i.e., fully two generations after Jesus' mission. More important, they were composed in response to the devastation of Judea and Jerusalem by the Romans in putting down the widespread revolt of 66-70 CE. Earlier texts such as Daniel and sections of *1 Enoch* were struggling to understand attacks on the traditional Judean way of life by the Hellenistic Seleucid empire but still expressed confidence that God was ultimately in control of history. 4 Ezra and 2 Baruch, however, address people who are in despair over the Roman imperial slaughter of their people and destruction of their society. Given

---

4. Daniel is available in the standard English Bibles, such as the NRSV or the New Jerusalem Bible; a good translation of the sections of *1 Enoch* now available is George Nickelsburg and James VanderKam, *1 Enoch: A New Translation* (Minneapolis: Fortress, 2004).

5. On Daniel and Enoch texts, see also Richard A. Horsley, *Scribes, Visionaries, and the Politics of Second Temple Judea* (Louisville: Westminster John Knox, 2007), chs. 8-9. On these and other texts, see also Horsley, *Revolt of the Scribes: Resistance and Apocalyptic Origins* (Minneapolis: Fortress, 2010).

6. It will not be possible adequately to explore this question here. See the caution voiced twenty-five years ago in Richard A. Horsley, *Jesus and the Spiral of Violence: Popular Jewish Resistance in Roman Palestine* (San Francisco: Harper & Row, 1987), pp. 129-43.

the different circumstances that they address, it makes sense to consider the later "apocalyptic" texts, which are sources for scribal reflection and hopes following the disastrous destruction of their society, separately from the second-temple Judean texts that are sources for beliefs and expectations in scribal circles before the time of Jesus.

"The End of the World"

Underlying the whole debate, but largely undiscussed with reference to Judean texts by either side, is the sense that the apocalyptic scenario is about the end of the world, the "cosmic catastrophe," as Bultmann put it. Borg and Crossan as well as Allison include Mark 13:24-25 (sun darkened, stars falling, etc.) in their citation of "apocalyptic son of man" texts. This has been a key "prooftext" for the "cosmic catastrophe" entailed in "the eschatological judgment." The scholarly belief that the scenario of apocalyptic eschatology meant the end of the world may have resulted from the overly literal reading of this passage and similar brief passages in only a few other texts. Interpreters have also failed to discern the roots of these images of cosmic disorder in prophetic tradition.

In the opening oracle of the Book of Watchers are several lines (*1 Enoch* 1:3-7) of images such as the mountains breaking apart and the earth rent asunder. Similarly, in the closing oracle of the *Testament of Moses* are several lines with such images as the earth shaken, the high mountains made low, the sun darkened, and the stars thrown into disarray (10:4-6). These images are hardly to be taken literally. They are part and parcel of a description of just how terrible it will be when "The Great Holy/Heavenly One" will come forth from the heavenly throne in judgment on the rebel heavenly "watchers and wicked deeds of humanity" or on "the nations." These passages, moreover, stand in a long tradition of *prophetic* oracles that announce "the day of Yahweh," God's coming to defeat oppressive rulers or the foreign kings who have conquered his people (e.g., Mic. 1:2-7; Jer. 25:30-38; Ezek. 32:5-8; Joel 2:10-11, 30-32; 3:14-15). As suggested by God's appearance on Sinai (*1 Enoch* 1:4), this prophetic portrayal of God's appearance in judgment was influenced by standard earlier portrayals of Yahweh's appearance with armies of holy ones from Sinai to deliver blessings on Israel and/or defeat enemy forces, as in the Blessing of Moses (see esp. Deut. 33:1-2, 27, 29) and the Song of Deborah (Judg. 5:4-5).

The point of the "earthshaking" images, in heightened metaphoric and hyperbolic language, was to symbolize how awesome would be the appearance of God in judgment. The whole tradition of such oracles was sharply political, pronouncing condemnation of oppressive domestic or foreign rulers and the people's deliverance from such rulers. In the oracle against imperial Babylon attributed to Isaiah, the traditional images of God's appearance in judgment are interspersed with a vivid portrayal of how devastating imperial warfare can be against the conquered populations (13:1-5, 6-10, 11-12, 13, 14-22). Yahweh coming in judgment against Babylon will "make the earth a desolation" — in attacks by the armies of the Medes (13:9, 17-18).[7] The prophetic oracle in Isaiah 24:17-23 even includes the "host of heaven" along with "the kings of the earth" in the divine punishment, a step toward the focus on judgment against the rebel watchers in the rest of the Book of Watchers. The language of mountains crumbling, earth shaking, and disarray in the heavenly bodies was not distinctively apocalyptic, but a prophetic tradition of God's judgment on oppressive imperial rulers, and it was not intended to be taken literally. In the other second-temple apocalyptic texts, there is nothing to suggest the end/destruction of the world. In fact, several texts have statements to the contrary, that the earth will be restored and/or that God will reign over all the earth (including *Testament of Moses* 10:1; the Book of Watchers, *1 Enoch* 11:18-22; and the Similitudes of Enoch, *1 Enoch* 45:4-5).

The view that "the end of the world" was central to Jewish apocalyp-

---

7. John J. Collins, "From Prophecy to Apocalypticism: The Expectation of the End," in *Encyclopedia of Apocalypticism*, vol. 1 (New York: Continuum, 2000), p. 130, believes that the language in Isaiah 13:9-13 "evokes a catastrophe of cosmic proportions. Thus, the notion of the end of this world has its origin in the cosmic imagery of Hebrew prophets in their oracles of destruction against specific places." Collins here evidently backs away from the standard way of reading the parallel lines of Hebrew poetry and prophecy such that they clarify each other or the second interprets the first. It is difficult to discern how one can construe Isaiah 13:9 — "to make the earth a desolation/and to destroy its sinners from it" — to mean a destruction of the world itself.

ticism still finds support in some of the current generation of scholarly specialists who have pioneered a more precise understanding of particular apocalyptic texts. John Collins, for example, argues that although no concept of the end of the world is evident, yet in the oracles of the prophets, their language, which "evokes a catastrophe of cosmic proportions, . . . underwent significant development in the period between the Babylonian Exile (586-539) and the rise of Christianity" that resulted in "the notion of the end of this world."[8] In the late second-temple texts he classifies as "historical apocalypses," however, he discusses only two brief passages that he claims envisage "the end of the world in a literal sense," and even those seem questionable.

His claim that in the ninth week of the "Apocalypse of Weeks" (*1 Enoch* 93:1-10; 91:11-17) "the world will be written down for destruction" (91:14)[9] is based on an older reconstruction of the text from one of the variants, which he seems to take literally. George Nickelsburg's more recent reconstruction of the text and translation give almost the opposite sense of the text: "a ninth week in which righteous law will be revealed to all the sons of the whole earth; and all the deeds of wickedness will vanish from the whole earth and descend into the eternal pit, and all humankind will look to the path of eternal righteousness."[10] Then the passing away of the first heaven and the appearance of a new heaven in the tenth week symbolize not the end of the world but restoration of the heavenly governance of the world, so that humankind can enjoy many "weeks" of life on the earth in piety and justice (91:15-17).

The other passage that Collins reads as attesting the end of the world, Daniel 12:1-3 (which he takes as "the end of days" in 12:13), is about the people being delivered from attacks and persecution by the emperor Antiochus Epiphanes, including the vindication of the martyred *maskilim*. As in the vision and interpretation of Daniel 7, with its similarly fantastic images, so in Daniel 10–12 the climactic focus is on the termination of imperial rule and the restoration of the people of Judea/Israel (12:1-3, on which see further below).

8. In his pivotal article "From Prophecy to Apocalypticism" in the *Encyclopedia of Apocalypticism*, vol. 1, pp. 129-30.

9. Collins, "From Prophecy to Apocalypticism," p. 140.

10. Nickelsburg, *1 Enoch 1*, p. 434.

It is surely significant that when Collins summarizes the worldview he finds implicit in second-temple apocalyptic texts he makes no mention of the concept of "the end of the world" and focuses instead on "the prominence of supernatural beings" and the new "hope of the individual" for "blessed immortality," for "glory with the angels," as a significant shift in Jewish spirituality.[11]

"Eschatological Judgment"

The portrayal of judgment varies from text to text. In the (third-century BCE) Book of Watchers (*1 Enoch* 1–36) it is clearly not eschatological, but is already being implemented, on the rebel heavenly "watchers" who were responsible for generating the race of giants that brought imperial warfare and exploitation. Most of the historical visions-and-interpretations focused on how to cope with the crisis of Seleucid imperial attacks and repression (Daniel 7; 8; 10–12; the Animal Vision, *1 Enoch* 85–90; the Ten-Week Vision, *1 Enoch* 93:1-10 + 91:11-17; *Testament of Moses*) have brief portrayals of judgment, along with renewal of Israel, at the very end. In these and the later Similitudes of Enoch (*1 Enoch* 37-69), the judgment is to be on the foreign empires/emperors who have oppressed and/or attacked the Judeans (e.g., Dan. 7:10-12, 26; 11:45 + 12:1a; *1 Enoch* 90:22-25; *Testament of Moses* 10:3, 7), although in some cases it includes the unfaithful Judean rulers who have cooperated with the imperial regimes (e.g., Dan. 12:2b?; *1 Enoch* 90:26-27). Judgment is urgent but not imminent, and it is future in these texts, but it does not seem to be eschatological in the sense of the end of history. It is rather expected as the resolution of the historical crisis that these texts address. The statement in Daniel 12:1a that "at that time Michael, the protector of your people, shall arise" as a high-ranking officer in the divine court is no exception. In the ongoing battles in the divine governance of historical affairs he has already been active fighting on behalf of the Judeans (Dan. 10:12-21). "At that time" in the future he will take more decisive action in the heavenly battle, presumably for the deliverance of the people from imperial rule. That is, in most of the second-

---

11. Collins, "From Prophecy to Apocalypticism," p. 147.

temple apocalyptic texts judgment is historical-political, and neither eschatological nor imminent.

In two of the Enoch texts judgment appears to be eschatological, not in the destruction of the world, but in the restoration of the world and fulfillment of history. The Ten-Week Vision has a historical judgment executed by the righteous against the wicked in the seventh week followed by an "everlasting judgment" executed on the (rebel) watchers in the tenth week. The passing away of the first heaven and appearance of a new heaven is eschatological, but it is not the end of the earth. It is rather the restoration of the heavenly governance of the earth where people will live in righteousness, similar to the restoration of the ideal conditions of creation following the judgment at the very end of the Animal Vision.

The "new heaven" as the symbol of restored divine governance of the earth suggests two important corrections of the misleading modern scholarly characterization of reality as imagined in apocalyptic texts. There is no "cosmic dualism." The heaven and the earth are included in the same cosmos. The earth is the place of historical life, including imperial kings who attack and oppress the people. Heaven(s) is the place of divine governance of earth and history, but a governance in which some of the heavenly forces are in rebellion against God's ultimate rule. The restoration of justice in earthly life is dependent on the resolution of the conflict(s) among the heavenly forces, of which the texts offer assurance. "Supernatural" and its counterpart "natural" are concepts from the modern western Enlightenment and scientific worldview that do not fit ancient Judean texts. The heavenly forces, such as the sun, moon, and stars, were superhuman and semi-divine, but not "supernatural" versus "natural."

"The Great Tribulation"

The scholarly impression that a "great tribulation" would be a principal event in the supposed "apocalyptic scenario" may be the result of tricks that their own translation and literal reading played on the scholars. There is no reference to a special time of tribulation or suffering in any of the second-temple apocalyptic texts, except for the brief statement in

Daniel 12:1b. But how should that reference be understood? That may depend on the relation of Daniel 12:1-3 to the vision-and-interpretation in Daniel 10–11. The book of Daniel is clearly a composite text, including three visions-and-interpretations in Daniel 7; 8; and 10–11 devoted mostly to lengthy accounts of the imperial oppression and attacks against the people followed by brief statements of the end of the emperor Antiochus Epiphanes. Daniel 7 has him destroyed, in 7:11, 26. Daniel 8 has him "broken" in a brief statement in 8:25. Daniel 10–11 ends with the briefest statement that "he shall come to his end, with no one to help him" (11:45). Because the relation of 12:1-3 to Daniel 10–11 is unclear, it is also unclear whether the "time of distress" refers to the severe recent attacks on people in Jerusalem already recounted in 11:31-35 (which are evidently continuing) or to a time more in the future. The reference to "since the nations/peoples came into existence" indicates that the distress or suffering is the result of political conflict, as in the attacks and persecutions already recounted in Daniel 11.

We noted in Chapter 3 that the "sufferings" mentioned in Mark 13:19, 24a (also) referred to the effects of Roman military attacks or acts of repression and persecution by Roman client rulers, i.e., to historical-political conflict and distress. In both Daniel 12:1b and Mark 13, on the basis of recent experience, the political repression was expected to become more severe before the people were delivered. In neither case, however, does it seem to refer to a special period of time in an eschatological scenario.

"Resurrection of the Dead"

Allison argued that Jesus must have simply presupposed resurrection as integral to the apocalypticism current in "Judaism" at the time.[12] But there are precious few references to resurrection of the dead in late second-temple Judean sources. Some of the prophetic passages previously claimed as attesting the resurrection of the dead (e.g., Ezek. 37; Isa. 26:16-19) are rather about the restoration of Israel. Some of the only (ap-

12. Dale C. Allison Jr., *Jesus of Nazareth* (Minneapolis: Fortress, 1998), p. 136; "Eschatology of Jesus," pp. 283-84.

parent) references to belief in the resurrection come from non-apocalyptic texts. In relation to their striving for righteousness and avoidance of sins the composers of the *Psalms of Solomon* believed that while "the destruction of the sinner is forever, . . . those who fear the Lord shall rise up to eternal life" (3:11-12), presumably a reference to resurrection. It has long been assumed, on the basis of Josephus' account (*War* 2.263), that the Pharisees, in contrast to the Sadducees, believed in the resurrection of the dead. The only reference to the resurrection in any of the second-temple apocalyptic texts is in Daniel 12:2, assuming that, as "sleep in the dust of the earth" refers to death, so "awake" refers to arising from the dead. The reference is brief and simple. It pertains to "your people" (12:1c), the Judeans. And the division of "to everlasting life" and "to everlasting contempt" is evidently between those who have remained faithful to the covenant and those who have not. It seems therefore that resurrection was not particularly important in second-temple apocalyptic texts and that it was not a distinctively apocalyptic belief.

The statement in Daniel 12:3 that "the wise shall shine . . . like the stars forever" has been taken as a reference to the resurrection of the dead. Its clear connection to "the wise" *(maskilim)* who have suffered martyr deaths because of their faithful adherence to the covenant in Daniel 11:33, however, indicates that the reference is to the divine vindication of the righteous for their faithfulness, and not specifically to the resurrection of the dead. The parallel imagery in the Epistle of Enoch (*1 Enoch* 104:2) similarly pertains to God's vindication of the righteous.

It seems unwarranted, on the basis of only Daniel 12:2, to take resurrection of the dead as a distinctively "apocalyptic" theme or event.

"Restoration of the People"

As mentioned above, this was not part of the apocalyptic scenario in the influential statements of Schweitzer and Bultmann. In fact, it did not fit; it would have seemed too "nationalistic" and historical to both. Allison introduced it, albeit in the limited form of the return of the exiled tribes, into his otherwise Schweitzerian restatement of the apocalyptic Jesus. Unfortunately for his claim, the theme of the return of the exiled tribes is not a concern of second-temple "apocalyptic" texts, which are focused on how to understand and endure the Hellenistic or Roman imperial invasion and oppression of Judea and Jerusalem.

The restoration of Judean society/Israel and of the people's independence in their land under God's direct rule, however, is one of the two key concerns of nearly all of these texts — in striking contrast with both "the Great Tribulation," which can hardly be said to appear even in Daniel 12:1b, and "the Resurrection of the Dead," which appears briefly only in Daniel 12:2. The restoration of the people is the usual companion theme to the judgment of the oppressive empire at the conclusion of most of these texts. It is the restoration of the people to sovereignty that the "one like a son of man" figure symbolizes in Daniel 7. Similarly it is the general point of Daniel 12:1-3 (in 12:1c). The resurrection of the dead and the vindication of "the wise" are particular aspects of the restoration. The renewal of the people follows directly upon the judgment of the imperial regimes and the wicked in the Animal Vision, with the universal restoration of creation tacked on at the end (*1 Enoch* 90:20-27, 28-36, 37-38). The renewal of the people follows upon the historical judgment in the Ten Week vision, before the universal restoration at the end (91:11, 13, 14-17). The glorious restoration of the people is the concluding event in the *Testament of Moses*, again paired with and following upon the judgment of the oppressive empire (10:3-7, 8-10). Far from being a component event of the standard "apocalyptic scenario" of the end of the world, however, the restoration of the people involves a continuation of historical life on the earth, and is often linked with a renewal of the world. What is more, the deliverance and restoration of the people/Israel is by no means an event/theme new or distinctive to apocalyptic texts. It had long been a standard and recurring concern of the prophets, both before and after the Babylonian destruction of Jerusalem and Judea. It is a dominant theme, for example, in the later sections of the book of Isaiah.

An "Apocalyptic Scenario"?

It is clear from Schweitzer's presentation that he and others at the beginning of the twentieth century were thinking of "apocalypticism" in terms of theological doctrine (dogma). After all, biblical studies (including its keen interest in Jewish apocalypticism and "the quest of the historical Jesus") was a branch of theology. Apocalyptic eschatology, for Schweitzer, was "dogmatic history" shaped by theological beliefs that would break in on ordinary, earthly history. Not surprisingly, apocalyptic eschatology was understood, in analogy with history, in terms of a sequence of "supernatural" events that would entail a cataclysmic end of worldly history.

The survey just above of the key events that supposedly comprised the "apocalyptic scenario" as presented by Schweitzer and Bultmann has shown that only judgment appears in most or all of the late second-temple Judean apocalyptic texts. The "coming Son of Man" as the agent of that judgment cannot be said to appear in any of them. In Daniel 7 the "one like a son of man" is a symbol for the restoration of the people, and in the Similitudes of Enoch "that son of man," like its synonym "the chosen one," is not a title, although the figure plays a role in the divine judgment. While the judgment may seem to be eschatological in two of the Enoch texts, in the sense of appearing at the fulfillment or climax of history, it is not imminent and is not "apocalyptic" as the end of the world. It rather leads to the renewal of the world as the place where the restored people can finally live in justice. The resurrection appears only in Daniel 12:2, among these apocalyptic texts, and does not appear to have been distinctively apocalyptic. The time of sufferings (that appears only) in Daniel 12:1b, like those in Mark 13:19, 24, appears to be historical-political, and not a special period or event in the end-of-the-world events. So there does not appear to have been a set or sequence of events that were eschatological in second-temple apocalyptic texts before or at the time of Jesus.

The only (brief) passage in any of these texts that might have suggested a sequence or "scenario" of "apocalyptic" events to scholars reading with "apocalyptic" assumptions is Daniel 12:1-3. In rapid succession come the great prince Michael arising (in the heavenly court of judgment, 12:1a), "a time of suffering" unprecedented in international relations (12:1b), and the restoration of the people (at least the faithful Judeans) found written in the book (used in divine judgment, 12:1c). Then come some particulars of that restoration of the people in the resurrection of some to life and some to contempt (12:2), and the vindication of the wise who had suffered martyrdom for faithfully resisting the persecution of Antiochus Epiphanes (they would "shine . . . like the stars," 12:3). While the resurrection-and-judgment that gives rewards to the faithful and unfaithful, respectively, in 12:2 seems to be a distinctive event, it is part of the judgment and restoration of the people declared in 12:1. Similarly, while the vindication of the martyrs who will shine like the stars appears to be a distinctive event, it too is part of the judgment and restoration of the people. Shining like the stars as vindication for the righteous at the divine judgment was a theme familiar in other scribal circles, as evident in the Epistle of Enoch (*1 Enoch* 104:2). Probably the reason it appears in Daniel 12:3 is that the *maskilim* who produced Daniel 10–12 were struggling to understand the martyrdom of some of their own scribal circle for resisting Antiochus Epiphanes.[13]

Daniel 12:1-3 thus appears to be a portrayal of the judgment of empire followed by the restoration of the people, parallel to the ending of several other second-temple apocalyptic texts, such as Daniel 7, the Animal Vision (*1 Enoch* 90:20-36), and the *Testament of Moses* (10). The close connection of God's judgment of oppressive foreign rulers and restoration of the people/Israel, however, is nothing new or distinctive to apocalyptic texts. The obvious combination of the defeat or judgment of oppressive rulers and the deliverance and restoration of the people was the focus of the victory songs of early Israel, such as the Song of the Sea and the Song of Deborah (Exod. 15; Judg. 5). It was also the focus of numerous prophetic oracles and particularly of late prophetic poems and oracles from earlier in the second-temple period — thus it cannot be categorized as particularly "apocalyptic."

Do 4 Ezra and 2 Baruch Attest the Apocalyptic Scenario?

Since "the apocalyptic scenario" of the end of the world does not appear in second-temple apocalyptic texts, where does it come from? One possi-

13. The *Testament of Moses* also includes an affirmation that God will vindicate (avenge) martyrs for their faithfulness under persecution (ch. 9). Then, in the oracle of judgment against imperial rule and restoration of the people (10:7-9), the image of shining like the stars seems to characterize the whole restored people, building on the representation of God's deliverance of Israel in the prophetic Song of Moses (Deut. 32:11-12).

bility is that something like this developed in the aftermath of the Roman devastation of Judea and Jerusalem in 69-70 CE and appears in 4 Ezra and 2 Baruch. The people who produced these texts are struggling with the disastrous destruction of Jerusalem and Judean society, struggling to summon some reassurance that God had not abandoned the people.

It is possible that the language of the old age and the new age and the old world and the new world in 4 Ezra (e.g., 4:26; 5:4-5; 6:7; 7:51; 8:1-2) was what led modern scholars to imagine that Jewish apocalypticism expected the end of the world. But these passages in some of the visions of 4 Ezra do not project imagery of destruction of the old age/world as transition to the new. Far from expecting some sort of cosmic catastrophe, 2 Baruch, while speaking of the world as corrupted and tired, imagines a renewed creation as the scene of an almost idyllic earthly life free of troubles (e.g., 40:3; 80:10; and 32:7; 57:2; 73).

4 Ezra is a series of seven visions-and-interpretations, each dealing with an urgent question or a dominant image of the resolution of the disastrous current situation of the destruction of Judean society. None of the events or themes of "the apocalyptic scenario" imagined by modern biblical scholars appear in the second vision (5:21–6:34), the fourth vision (9:26–10:59, dealing with the bereft woman replaced by the new Jerusalem), the fifth vision (chapters 11-12, about the eagle [the terribly destructive Roman imperial rule] confronted by the lion [the anointed one]), or the seventh vision (ch. 14). It is also difficult to find any of the events of the supposed apocalyptic scenario in the sixth vision (ch. 13) about "the man from the sea," i.e., the anointed one, who achieves victory over the attacking nations, not by weapons of war but by the fire/word of his mouth (as in Psalm of Solomon 17). This vision mentions explicitly the restoration of the people, including the return of the ten dispersed tribes (13:40-45), which was asserted by Allison but was inconsistent with the scenario articulated by Schweitzer and Bultmann. None of the visions mention "the son of man" explicitly, although the appearance of the anointed figure in the sixth vision alludes to the "coming with the clouds" (13:3).

The first vision (3:1–5:20, concerning why the evil "Babylon" has conquered God's people and for "how long") finds "signs" of the eventual time of deliverance in what could have been read as the time of tribulation. Similarly, the third vision (6:35–9:25, again asking "how long" and "when") finds "signs" in a vision of future sufferings and disarray in the heavenly bodies associated with God coming in deliverance (8:50; 9:2-8), which may have been taken as the time of great tribulation. This vision, alone in 4 Ezra, also refers at least briefly to the judgment (7:32-44, 70, 102-4, 113) and to the resurrection of the dead connected with the judgment (7:32, 37), and speculates on the pre-resurrection condition of the dead (7:75-101). It would be difficult to argue, however, that the third vision presupposes or articulates a "scenario" of (linked or sequential) events as represented by Schweitzer and Bultmann.

Most striking about 4 Ezra is the diversity of images of the future in which God and/or the anointed one would act to end the imperial devastation that is so difficult to understand. While these images do not include a "son of man" figure, they do include the anointed figure that had not appeared in second-temple apocalyptic texts.

2 Baruch, which ranges over many issues and topics, does have a section on sufferings in connection with the question of "when" or "how long" (chapters 25–27) and a reference to international historical events (70:8-9) that scholars may have taken as references to the time of tribulation. It also includes two brief discussions of resurrection (30:1-5; 50:2-3; 51). Curiously, reference to the judgment crops up rarely (57:2), even if reference to defeat of the imperial rulers is included in judgment (70:7). This lengthy text simply does not seem to presuppose, much less to articulate, the supposed "apocalyptic scenario."

Conclusion

This survey both of second-temple Judean apocalyptic texts and of the later 4 Ezra and 2 Baruch thus shows that they do not articulate or presuppose an "apocalyptic scenario" of key themes or events any more than do the sayings of Jesus or of John the Baptist. Rather apocalyptic texts, both those that address the historical crises posed by imperial rulers' attacks on second-temple Jerusalem and the later ones struggling to deal with the destruction of Jerusalem and the people, focus on the future judgment of oppressive empires and the restoration of the people by God.

CHAPTER FIVE

Tilting at the Apocalyptic Windmill

The legendary Don Quixote, a carryover from the bygone era of knighthood, continued to do battle with fearsome dragons. He could not see that the dragons against which he was tilting were mere windmills. The prominent recent debates over the apocalyptic Jesus appear to be a somewhat similar story. Liberal scholars, still operating on the assumptions of an earlier era, are doing battle against the dragon(s) of the apocalyptic scenario that they believe has been holding the historical Jesus captive. In the recent scholarly jousting, however, other noble knights, also operating on the old assumptions, rise to the defense of what the liberals see as a dragon, but what they see as the real historical Jesus.

A Diversionary Debate

In recent debate over whether Jesus was apocalyptic, both sides agree on and work with the standard older view of Jewish apocalyptic eschatology more or less as articulated a century ago by Schweitzer and summarized a generation later by Rudolf Bultmann. Both sides agree that John the Baptist, Paul, and other early Christians shared this worldview. The only question is whether Jesus did or did not believe and preach apocalyptic eschatology, at the center of which was the "apocalyptic scenario" of the "end of the world," of a "cosmic catastrophe," of imminent eschatological judgment, carried out by the Son of Man, preceded by the great tribulation, and followed by an otherworldly resurrection existence.

The surveys in Chapters 2 and 3 show that the individual sayings of Jesus or John adduced as evidence that he or John did or did not preach the key themes of the apocalyptic scenario do not attest what scholars claim. The survey in Chapter 4 shows, moreover, that, except for a divine judgment that is not imminent or eschatological, the key events of the apocalyptic scenario as presented by Schweitzer and Bultmann and assumed by subsequent scholars do not appear much at all in second-temple apocalyptic texts. Resurrection and sufferings that might be taken as the tribulation appear in only two of the visions in the later 4 Ezra. The whole scenario is not attested in any of these texts.

We may thus begin to suspect that "the apocalyptic scenario" assumed in modern scholarly discussions of Jesus is a construct of modern scholars. Allison seems to be aware of this in his reference to "the conventional paradigm of Jesus as eschatological prophet" that derives from Schweitzer and Johannes Weiss, who had previously painted a highly similar picture of Jesus' preaching. How Schweitzer developed his own picture of the apocalyptic Jesus confirms the impression. He was fully aware of how "intermittent" Jewish apocalyptic literature was, from Daniel (early second century BCE) to 4 Ezra (early second century CE). Assuming that the Baptist, Jesus, and Paul all fully shared the apocalyptic worldview, however, he believed it justified to reconstruct the Jewish apocalypticism of Jesus' time directly out of Matthew, Mark, and Paul.

In retrospect, therefore, it seems likely that the apocalyptic scenario presented by Schweitzer and assumed by many Jesus interpreters ever since was constructed on the basis of motifs and images from the Gospels and Paul, for which scholars found "parallels" scattered here and there in words, images, and verses from various Jewish apocalyptic texts. One can see in Schweitzer's presentation of Jesus how passages in Matthew, such as Jesus' explanation of the parable of the tares (13:17-43), the picture of the *palingenesia* (19:28), and key sayings in the *parousia* discourse (24:3-4, 8, 21, 29-31, 36-44; 25:31-33, 46), influenced the construction of Jewish apocalypticism generally and the "apocalyptic scenario" in particular.

To see how influential scholars of a century ago proceeded we need look no farther than Schweitzer's predecessor in the presentation of the apocalyptic Jesus, Johannes Weiss.[1] A critical scholar, Weiss excludes certain sources (John) and sorts out sayings that he judges secondary (e.g., Mark 9:1 and Matt. 13:37, 43, 47-50). With what passed critical muster, however, he makes remarkable synthetic combinations out of sayings and even words taken literally and out of literary context. In a long paragraph on "how Jesus conceived the events related to God's establishment of the Kingdom," for example, he combines verses, lines, images, and individual words from a wide variety of texts, including Revelation 6:12-17; 2 Peter 3:10; 1 Corinthians 15:50, 52; and 4 Ezra 4:26ff., as well as the "parousia" speeches in the Synoptic Gospels. From "the parousia speech" in Luke 17:22-37 he finds that the appearance of the Son of Man will be sudden but also (more importantly) universal and destructive (analogous to the flood). More decisive than the wars and insurrection, among "all these things happening" in "the other parousia saying" sifted out of Mark 13, is "the breakup of the old world" in 13:24-25a, also described "exactly" in Revelation 6:12-17, which will include the destruction of the Temple. Everything must become new (Rev. 21:1, 4; 2 Peter 3:10), which had already been expressed by the Jewish author of 4 Ezra (4:26ff. — "this age" and the new "field," which Weiss reads not only literally but metaphysically). This, he claims, is what Jesus meant in the word *palingenesia* (Matt. 19:28); he too expected "a new heaven and new earth." To participate in this transformation, the people who are to live in this Kingdom must also be transformed, casting off their old nature of flesh and blood (1 Cor. 15:50; 4 Ezra 4:11), to become like the angels in heaven, exalted above all earthly needs (*1 Enoch* 15:3-7), as Jesus (had supposedly) stated positively (Matt. 22:30; Mark 12:25). All of this is remarkably similar to, indeed a precursor of, the apocalyptic scenario laid out by Schweitzer. It is a synthetic tour de force, eclectic in the extreme, and not derived primarily from Jewish apocalyptic texts.

A review of the understanding of apocalypticism in German biblical studies and theology forty years ago noted that after a translation of an-

---

1. The following illustration is a summary of the presentation in Johannes Weiss, *Jesus' Proclamation of the Kingdom of God*, trans. Richard Hiers and David Holland from the first German edition of 1892 (Philadelphia: Fortress, 1971), pp. 92-96.

cient Jewish apocalyptic texts and two handbooks on Jewish apocalypticism appeared around 1900, no scholarly attention was devoted to the texts and the subject until around 1960.[2] More critical study and (re-)interpretation of Judean apocalyptic texts in the U.S. did not begin until the 1970s.[3] With the increasing specialization in the field of biblical studies, however, it has evidently not been possible for interpreters of the historical Jesus to appropriate this more sophisticated recent work on particular apocalyptic texts or to work from the recent new translations of the texts themselves. The standard way of dealing with such texts, moreover, has remained to focus on text fragments of an image, a motif, or at most a few lines.[4] In effect, both sides of the debate are still working with an understanding of apocalyptic that has changed little since the late nineteenth century.

The implications of the above survey for the recent debate about the apocalyptic Jesus would seem to be fairly obvious. Since the sayings of Jesus (or John) presented as evidence of the events or themes of the apocalyptic scenario do not attest them, and they are not much in evidence in Judean apocalyptic texts, the apocalyptic scenario assumed by Jesus scholars must be a modern scholarly construct. The debate about whether Jesus was an apocalyptic preacher is not about the historical Jesus in a cultural context attested by Judean apocalyptic texts. The debate is rather about a *synthetic modern scholarly construct* of Judaism and Jesus and early Christianity. Scholarly discussion about the apocalyptic Jesus is a diversionary debate. What the liberals are tilting against and others defending can now, more realistically, be seen to be the construction of previous generations of scholars. That being the case, the historical Je-

2. Klaus Koch, *Ratlos vor der Apokalyptik,* translated as *The Rediscovery of Apocalyptic* (SBT 2/22; Naperville, IL: Allenson, 1972), p. 13.

3. Two of the leading specialists, who began publishing groundbreaking articles on particular texts in the 1970s, produced more general book-length treatments in the early 1980s: George Nickelsburg, *Jewish Literature from the Bible to the Mishnah,* 1st ed. (Philadelphia: Fortress, 1981); and John J. Collins, *The Apocalyptic Imagination* (New York: Crossroad, 1983).

4. John Dominic Crossan, a notable exception, cites larger text-fragments (in *Jesus: A Revolutionary Biography* [New York: HarperOne, 1994], pp. 106-10), yet still presupposes the standard scholarly scenario and its themes, and even includes the *Psalms of Solomon* in his standard synthetic construct of apocalyptic eschatology.

sus cannot have been an apocalyptic preacher breathing the fire of eschatological judgment. Nor was "apocalypticism" the fearsome fire-breathing dragon from which liberals had to rescue a Jesus more compatible with modern sensitivities.

The modern scholarly construct of apocalypticism, however, may be a good illustration of how biblical studies in general, including investigation of the historical Jesus in particular, operates. The understanding of text-fragments and historical figures and events is guided or (perhaps more accurately) determined by a number of synthetic and often essentialist concepts that have been developed in the modern field of biblical studies. "(Early) Judaism" and "(early) Christianity" are the broadest. These broad synthetic concepts are often anachronistic; at the time of Jesus or Paul or the Judean historian Josephus, there was no such thing as (early) Judaism or (early) Christianity. Neither had yet emerged so as to be identifiable as what is denoted or connoted in these modern concepts. These modern constructs also hide or obscure the particulars of texts, society, and history.

In order to approach and begin to understand the historical Jesus in the historical context of ancient Galilee and Judea, it is necessary to get "underneath" such misleading concepts or perhaps, more realistically, to work consciously not to let them continue to determine our understanding. Since we depend largely on extant texts for our knowledge of the society and culture in which Jesus and his followers lived, we presumably want to reread those texts undetermined by broad synthetic modern constructs such as "apocalypticism" and "wisdom." And texts we have categorized as "apocalyptic" are some of our principal sources for what was happening in ancient Judea in the centuries prior to (and somewhat after) the time of Jesus. Taking apocalyptic texts as an important historical source, it makes sense to read particular texts to see what they are about.

What Apocalyptic Texts Are About

Most of the second-temple Judean texts that have been classified as "apocalyptic" take more or less the same form of "vision-and-interpretation."

They consist largely of a review of previous history leading up to an acute historical crisis in Judea (that involves the composers). They conclude with a shorter future resolution of the crisis in God's judgment of the empire that is oppressing the people and renewal of the people of Judea and/or of all people. The visions and interpretations in Daniel 7, 8, and 10–12 (easily accessible to any reader) review the increasingly violent oppression of Judeans by the Persian and especially the Hellenistic empires, climaxing in the invasion of Judea and Jerusalem by Antiochus Epiphanes. The Animal Vision and Ten-Week Vision in the book of *1 Enoch* (chapters 85–90 and 93:2-20 + 91:11-17, respectively, also now readily accessible)[5] review history since the creation but focus on the increased oppression of Judeans under the Hellenistic empires. In the vision of Daniel 7 the empires are symbolized by vicious predatory beasts. In "Enoch's" Animal Vision the violent treatment of the people is symbolized by beasts and birds of prey under the higher power of "shepherds" (imperial rulers) who exceed the authority given them by God as overall Lord of history. In all of these texts, the oppression has become severe under the harsh rule of Antiochus Epiphanes, who has invaded to enforce the breaking of the covenant by the Judean rulers (their Hellenizing "reform"). They all end, in the confidence that the Most High is still in control of history, in a judgment on the rulers and a restoration of the Judean people (Israel), to which the two "Enoch" texts add a restoration of the earth and renewal of all people under restored heavenly rule.

Far from being "alienated" from history which they anticipate coming to an End in a cosmic cataclysm, they are focused on how imperial rule has become intolerably oppressive and increasingly violent in suppression of the traditional Judean way of life. The composers are struggling to understand how history can have gotten so "out of control" under the succession of empires to which they have been subjected. Part of the historical crisis is that their own high-priestly rulers have been cooperating with imperial rule in violation of the covenant. The review of history in Daniel 10–12 sees them as having abandoned the covenant (11:28-32). The Animal Vision views the "tower," which symbolizes the second

---

5. A fine translation of the sections of *1 Enoch* is available in George Nickelsburg and James VanderKam, *1 Enoch: A New Translation* (Minneapolis: Fortress, 2004).

Temple, as illegitimate, having "polluted bread on its table" (*1 Enoch* 89:73). The people who composed these visions-and-interpretations of history were also engaged in resistance against the invasion of the emperor and suppression of the traditional way of life, even to the point of having been martyred (Dan. 11:32-35; *1 Enoch* 90:6-19; 91:11). The resolution of the crisis of severe imperial oppression is anticipated to come with the end of empire (not the end of the world) in the divine judgment. In the best-known portrayal of the judgment, in Daniel 7, "the one like a son of man coming with the clouds of heaven" is a visionary symbol that is explained as referring to the granting of dominion to "the people of the holy ones of the Most High," i.e., the Judeans (Israel).

Who Produced Apocalyptic Texts?

It was understandable that Schweitzer, Bultmann, and subsequent interpreters of Jesus still working within the synthetic modern constructs could have believed that "apocalypticism" was prominent, perhaps pervasive in "Judaism." Before the discovery of the Dead Sea Scrolls, "apocalyptic" texts were some of the only sources available for "Judaism" within one or two hundred years of the time of Jesus. If we abandon such essentialist concepts for a closer look at late second-temple Judean society, however, we can ascertain more precisely how texts classified as apocalyptic may be related to Jesus and his followers.[6]

"The wise among the people," some of whom were being martyred in Daniel 11:33; 12:3, were evidently the people who produced the visions-and-interpretations of Daniel 7, 8, and 10–12. The scribes who produced the Animal Vision and other texts collected in *1 Enoch* represented "Enoch" as a learned scribe who possesses wisdom as well as the ability to read and write, and as the recipient of special revealed wisdom. Those who produced the books of wisdom that were revealed to "Enoch" were thus evidently representing their heavenly source in their own image.

---

6. The following builds on and is a summary of the historical-social-cultural investigation in Horsley, *Scribes, Visionaries, and the Politics of Second Temple Judea* (Louisville: Westminster John Knox, 2007).

"Daniel" and his Judean companions, moreover, are represented as "trained in every branch of wisdom" so that they are qualified to serve in the court of the Persian emperor (Dan. 1:3-7).

We might already have a sense of the "social location" and "role" of "the wise" or learned scribes from reading the Gospels, where the scribes (and Pharisees) "come down from Jerusalem" to the villages of Galilee as representatives of the high-priestly rulers and are closely associated with the high priests in Jerusalem. The wise scribe Jesus ben Sira, whose instructional and other kinds of wisdom are collected in the book of Sirach (Ecclesiasticus), offers a clear sense of where learned scribes fit in the political-economic structure of the Judean temple-state. In a long speech lauding the role of the scribe, he mentions the various artisans and the plowmen on whose labor a city (Jerusalem) depends. Yet only the scribe has the leisure to study the Torah of the Most High, learn prophecies, and acquire the wisdom of the ancients so that he can serve among the rulers in councils of state (Sir. 38:24–39:11). In other instructional speeches, Ben Sira urges his scribal protégés to sympathize with and even defend the poor who are exploited by the high-priestly rulers. But the scribes understand themselves as socially and culturally superior to the people. And although they are critical of the wealthy and powerful for exploiting the poor, they are themselves clearly dependent on the favor of the high-priestly rulers (among) whom they serve as advisers knowledgeable in the Torah of God, prophecies, and various kinds of wisdom.

Among the various kinds of wisdom that Daniel and his friends, and presumably Ben Sira and his protégés, cultivated were cosmological wisdom, about the revolution of the heavenly bodies and the weather, and "mantic" wisdom, including interpretation of dreams in order to understand historical events. As Ben Sira notes, the learned scribes also cultivated prophecies, the oracles of the earlier Israelite prophets. "Daniel" is portrayed as a remarkable interpreter of dreams, and the very form taken by most of the texts we classify as "apocalyptic" was vision-and-interpretation, as noted just above. It seems clear that some of the same learned scribes who produced wisdom of the kind found in Sirach, Proverbs, Ecclesiastes, and Job also (or instead) produced texts such as Daniel 7, 8, 10–12, and the Animal Vision and Ten-Week Vision. When some of their high-priestly patrons began collaborating with the emperor, who invaded Jerusalem in support of their "reform," some of "the wise" scribes resorted to their knowledge of dream interpretation and cosmological wisdom to understand the historical crisis and their own persecution. According to their visions-and-interpretations, God was still in control of history and would judge the empire and restore the people.

The Relationship Between Scribal Texts and the People

Since, as Jesus ben Sira states, Jerusalem artisans and Judean farmers lacked the leisure to cultivate wisdom, it would seem that the "apocalyptic" texts, like other scribal texts, would not be good sources for their views and attitudes. Under the attacks by Antiochus Epiphanes, however, "the wise" who produced Daniel 10–12 said that "the wise among the people shall give understanding to many" as they were martyred by imperial violence. It is difficult to tell exactly what this may have meant. Did it mean that their martyrdom would inspire the many to join in the resistance? Did it mean that in the crisis "the wise" scribes, who did not regularly associate with the ordinary Jerusalemites, would suddenly become missionaries? As "the wise" suddenly, under intensified imperial domination of Jerusalem, came to experience the kind of oppression that villages experienced from their rulers on a regular basis, did their interpretation of the historical crisis come to reflect, or at least parallel, popular attitudes? It may have meant any or all of those things.

On the other hand, some of Jesus' statements in the Gospels suggest that there was more of a gulf between scribal texts and the views of the people. The Gospels portray a general and persistent conflict between Jesus and his followers, on the one hand, and the scribes and Pharisees, on the other. Particularly striking are Jesus' prophetic woes and other statements condemning them for their role in economic exploitation of the people by draining their locally needed subsistence produce for support of the Temple (Mark 7:1-13; 12:38-44; Luke 11:39-52; see further Chapter 10). It is difficult to find in the Gospels, moreover, anything that resembles the kind of scribal lore that appears in several apocalyptic texts.

Apocalyptic Texts as Sources for the
Historical Context of the Historical Jesus

Apocalyptic texts are nevertheless very important as sources for the historical context in which Jesus lived and worked. The scribal visions-and-interpretations "reveal" that the overarching, determinative reality in late second-temple Judea was Hellenistic and then Roman imperial rule. As indicated in the books of Ezra, Nehemiah, Haggai, and Zechariah, the Persian imperial regime had sponsored the rebuilding of the Temple as the institution to which Judeans sent tithes and offerings to "the god who is in Jerusalem." As the restored rulers of the temple-state, the high-priestly aristocracy dutifully sent tribute to the imperial capital and maintained the imperial order in Judea. The successor empires continued the arrangement, in which the high-priestly families were subservient to and dependent on the imperial regime to maintain their power and privileged position. The Similitudes of Enoch (*1 Enoch* 37–71), the "apocalyptic" text dated closest to the time of Jesus, indicates clearly that the principal problem for the people of Roman Palestine was still "the kings and the powerful" who controlled the people and their land.

In what may now seem like the recent claim of a "clash of civilizations" between "western civilization" and the Islamist orient, the rise of "apocalypticism" and the Maccabean Revolt with which it was often linked have been explained as a clash between a cosmopolitan "Hellenism" and reactionary parochial "Judaism." This explanation is rooted in the old essentialist cultural constructs that simplify and distort historical relationships and developments that are/were much more complicated. A major aspect of the historical crises evident in Judean apocalyptic texts was clearly the attempt to impose "western" Hellenistic political-cultural forms onto indigenous Judean society. But this was only the cultural-religious aspect of the more fundamental political-economic-cultural divide between the Hellenistic and later the Roman imperial rulers and their clients/allies in Jerusalem, on the one hand, and the Judeans committed to their traditional way of life, including several circles of scribes, on the other. Complicated somewhat by the Romans, who appointed Herodian rulers above or parallel to the high-priestly rulers in Jerusalem, this fundamental divide between rulers and ruled continued through the end of the second-temple period. At the time of Jesus, the Roman governor appointed the high priests, and the high-priestly aristocracy was responsible for collecting the Roman tribute from the villagers.

Just how serious this fundamental division was for Judeans and, surely, other Israelites who lived in Galilee and Samaria as well, is indicated by the very composition of the visions-and-interpretations we call apocalyptic and the scribal resistance they attest. Even though learned scribes were the professional advisers and representatives of the high-priestly rulers in Jerusalem and economically dependent on them, some scribes turned to resistance to imperial rule (and their own patrons) when they felt it threatened the traditional Judean covenantal way of life. Their commitment to the Judean cultural heritage and the societal life for which it supposedly provided the guidance overcame their vulnerability to the priestly aristocracy that they served. That their opposition to the imperial rulers entailed their opposition to the incumbent high-priestly rulers is indicated in several of the apocalyptic texts, as noted. The (non-apocalyptic) series of prophetic woes in the Epistle of Enoch (*1 Enoch* 94–105) illustrate how vehemently they could condemn the wealthy and powerful Jerusalem rulers for their exploitation of the people. Sometime in mid-second century BCE, when the Hasmonean brothers who had led the Maccabean Revolt negotiated their own recognition as high priests in Jerusalem, another circle of scribes and priests withdrew to the wilderness in adamant protest and formed the community at Qumran that left the Dead Sea Scrolls. Although they may not have regularly associated with Jerusalem artisans and Judean villagers, at least several circles of scribes turned against, condemned, and resisted both the imperial rulers and the client rulers in Jerusalem.

All of the scribes and the political factions that emerged among them, the Pharisees, the Sadducees, and what Josephus calls the "fourth philosophy," amounted to only a tiny fraction of the population of Judea. It is not clear whether any of them were ever active in Galilee, which was not taken over by the Jerusalem high-priestly rulers until 104 BCE and was not under Jerusalem jurisdiction during the lifetime of Jesus. So we need to look to other sources for more direct access to the life of the Judean and Galilean people. Because literacy was limited to a tiny minority (the cultural elite, which in Judea were the scribal circles), the nonliterate people almost never left sources that at some point were written down and survived. The Gospels are unusual, indeed almost unique, as textual sources from and for the movement(s) that formed from among the followers of Jesus. But we must think critically and carefully about how the Gospels can be used as sources and think critically about what we are looking for in Jesus as a leader who became historically significant.

PART II

The Prophet of Renewal:
Jesus in Historical Context

CHAPTER SIX

Toward a Relational Jesus in Historical Context

Investigation and interpretation of "the historical Jesus" has developed as a subfield of New Testament studies, which developed as a subdivision of theology. This is vividly evident in Schweitzer's statement that "eschatology is simply 'dogmatic history' — history as moulded by theological beliefs — which breaks in upon the natural course of history and abrogates it."[1] It may thus not be surprising that the concrete circumstances, agents, interactions, conflicts, and other processes of history become obscured by assumptions, approaches, and concepts that became standard in New Testament studies, so heavily influenced by theology. Books on the historical Jesus continue to betray their roots in those well-established assumptions and methods. Many of the assumptions, methods, and concepts standard in historical Jesus studies are very different from those of historians involved in the investigation of other historical figures and movements. Serious critical reflection seems to be in order, reflection that will require extensive analysis. As a provisional step, we can focus here on two principal concerns: recognition and assessment of the Gospel sources for Jesus; and working toward a more relational and contextual approach.

---

1. Albert Schweitzer, *The Quest of the Historical Jesus* (New York: Macmillan, 1961), p. 351.

The Gospel Sources

One of the first and most basic responsibilities of historians is to critically evaluate the sources for historical figures and events, including how they can and cannot be used. In the standard critical approach to the historical Jesus the assumption, for at least the last hundred years, has been that the sources (of the "data") for (re-)construction of the historical Jesus are the individual sayings or brief stories contained in the Gospels. The latter have been taken as mere containers or collections or compilations of the sayings of Jesus and the story-vignettes about him or his brief debates. The earliest Gospel, Mark, was viewed as analogous to a string of beads. Scholars focused on the individual beads, mainly the sayings.

It is likely that the codification of the Gospel texts into chapter and verse, along with the appearance of each verse separately on the pages of the Lutherbibel (in Germany) and the King James Version (in Britain and the U.S.) influenced this atomizing approach. The most powerful impetus for the crystallization of the focus on the individual sayings of Jesus, however, probably came from the Enlightenment that had given rise to interest in "the historical Jesus" in the first place. Enlightenment Reason also sharpened critical biblical scholars' sense of what seemed to be the "supernatural" or "irrational" worldview evident in the Gospel narratives, which stood in stark contrast to the modern scientific understanding of reality. The Enlightenment reduction of reality to fit the canons of Reason and Nature left theologians, including New Testament scholars, embarrassed about the Christian Gospels as sources for the historical Jesus. There was altogether too much of the fantastic and "miraculous" in the Gospel stories. By the late nineteenth century critical theologians also recognized that the Gospel "writers" had provided the overall framing of the Gospel stories from their own faith perspectives, rooted in their conviction about Jesus' resurrection. The only reliable materials that could meet modern scientific criteria for historical evidence were the teachings of Jesus, which they had come to assume consisted of individual sayings. Understandably, scholars who were attempting to attain a sense of the historical Jesus proceeded by isolating individual sayings from their faith-framing and to test them by various criteria for their "authenticity."

Support for the focus on the individual sayings of Jesus came from the hypothesis that the close verbal parallels between the non-Markan teachings of Jesus in Matthew and Luke must mean that they had used a common source (*Quelle* in German, usually shortened to "Q" as the designation of this material). On the assumption that Jesus' teaching took the form of individual sayings, this was taken as a (mere) "collection" of individual sayings, and designated "the Synoptic Sayings Source." The discovery of the *Gospel of Thomas*, which had the form, in manuscript, of a seemingly random collection of individual or double sayings or parables, strongly reinforced the standard assumption about the form of the teaching on which the (re-)construction of the historical Jesus was focused. The self-selecting regular gathering of scholars in the Jesus Seminar proceeded precisely by focusing on the individual sayings of Jesus, further refining the "form-critical" approach started by Bultmann. But many other critical interpreters of Jesus continued to focus on the isolated individual sayings of Jesus (as indicated in Chapter 3 above). Critical interpreters of Jesus, such as Crossan, Funk, and John Meier, affirm that Jesus also performed healings and exorcisms. But they find little reliable evidence in the "miracle stories" that any of the healings and exorcisms "go back to" Jesus himself, leaving the focus all the more on the individual sayings.[2]

This assumption about the atomistic form of Jesus' teaching and this standard procedure of focusing on individual sayings of Jesus, however, are acutely problematic. The most obvious problem is the historical impossibility of anyone *communicating* intelligibly with other people only or mainly in isolated individual sayings. Proverbs and other aphorisms may be gathered into collections, such as certain sections of the book of Proverbs. But proverbs have meaning or rhetorical effect only when applied in some context. To have become a historically significant

---

2. Robert W. Funk and the Jesus Seminar, *The Acts of Jesus: The Search for the Authentic Deeds of Jesus* (San Francisco: HarperSanFrancisco, 1998); and John O. Meier, *A Marginal Jew: Rethinking the Historical Jesus*, vol. 2: *Mentor, Message, and Miracles* (New York: Doubleday, 1994) devote hundreds of pages to searching the miracle stories for elements that "go back to Jesus," yet pay little attention to the historical context of illness and healing or spirit-possession and exorcism, and devote little attention to the understanding of healing and exorcism in the historical context.

figure, Jesus would presumably have been communicating with other people. But individual sayings do not constitute meaningful units of communication.

A second, closely related problem is that the meaning of a saying or story always depends on a meaning-context. The standard scholarly practice of taking the sayings of Jesus out of their literary context leaves the modern interpreters with no indication from the historical context as to their meaning. Like museum curators of a generation or two ago, scholarly interpreters of Jesus arrange decontextualized artifacts by type ("apocalyptic" or "sapiential") and/or topic (children, meals, kingdom, wisdom), like pottery fragments unearthed in archeological digs displayed in museum cases (fragments of lamps, vases, pots, jars).[3] The topical arrangement of Jesus' sayings by scholarly interpreters in the chapters of books about Jesus has only the most general relation to the historical circumstances in which Jesus lived. Isolated individual sayings of Jesus may be precious artifacts to the archeologist-like scholars who sort them out and categorize them, but they do not by themselves contain or convey meaning, and they beg the question of context.

The result is a Jesus who uttered artifact-like aphorisms, but was not communicating something significant to particular people in a concrete historical situation, i.e., a dehistoricized "talking head" unattached to any particular life-circumstances. Scholars thus generate a larger or smaller "database" of atomized Jesus sayings without meaning-context. The meaning-context is then supplied by the modern interpreter(s), often from the discourse of modern biblical scholarship, as illustrated in Chapters 2 and 3 above. Crossan supplies the vengeful judgment of God from the modern construct of apocalypticism to John the Baptist's utter-

3. The recent application of the analogy of archeological "excavations" and their determination of the "strata" at the sites suggests that this may be the way some scholars of the Gospels or the historical Jesus understand their investigations, as "excavating Jesus" or "excavating Q." The analogy also suggests that the very dead Jesus now exists only in artifacts recently excavated from piles of dirt obstructing those precious fragments of his teaching. The current generation of archeologists, however, not only attempts to discern how the fragments comprised a whole pot or vase, but attempts to discern how pots, fire pits, houses, and courtyards comprised whole villages. Correspondingly, recent museum exhibits tend to display particular artifacts in the broader context of a house or village.

ance about the winnowing fork and fire. Allison lists sets of Jesus' sayings as evidence of the themes of the apocalyptic scenario consciously taken from Weiss and Schweitzer — following in a long tradition of theologians, from John Calvin on, who listed "prooftexts" for whichever theological doctrine they were expounding.

A third problem has recently become clear to other biblical scholars but evidently not yet to many interpreters of Jesus. As just noted, scholars focused on individual sayings of Jesus treat the Gospels as mere containers or collections, and ignore the Gospels themselves as potential sources. In the last generation, however, we have come to recognize the Gospels as whole stories about Jesus and the movement(s) he catalyzed. The Gospel stories, moreover, consist not of unrelated sayings and ministories, but of a sequence of interrelated episodes and longer or shorter speeches on various issues. Indeed, the teachings not in Mark but closely parallel in Matthew and Luke ("Q") take the form of speeches, not separate sayings. To a considerable extent this can be discerned in the arrangements of Jesus' teaching on the pages of recent translations, such as the NRSV and the New Jerusalem Bible — although the topical headings were supplied by modern editors, and not in the Greek text that has been constructed by modern scholars. Furthermore, the Gospels portray Jesus communicating and interacting with people and as coming into conflict particularly with the rulers and their representatives. The Gospels, moreover, portray him interacting with people in particular social contexts such as houses, village communities, their local assemblies (synagogues), and the Temple in Jerusalem. The interaction, moreover, including people's response to his speech or action, is an important factor in what happens. The Gospels thus portray Jesus as a historical actor or agent, and not as an unengaged individual teacher who utters individual sayings and aphorisms.

The Gospels, as stories and speeches, are our principal historical sources for the historical Jesus. As critical scholars of the nineteenth century recognized, of course, we cannot read the "life" of Jesus directly from the surface of the texts of the Gospels. The challenge, and one of our principal responsibilities as historians, is to figure out how to use the Gospels critically as sources for the historical Jesus in context. To this we will return in Chapter 8 below.

Jesus-in-Movement-in-Context

First, however, it is necessary to move beyond another crippling problem in the standard approach to the historical Jesus that calls for a far more elaborate and comprehensive critique than we can carry out here. But we can perhaps, in a provisional way, discern some of the contours of a more adequate, relational, and contextual approach to Jesus as a significant historical figure.

A major obstacle to more adequately understanding the historical Jesus is the individualism that dominates modern western culture, particularly American culture. Most interpreters of Jesus simply assume this individualism and project it onto Jesus. Schweitzer's apocalyptic Jesus, reasserted by Allison and others, stands apart as a lone, isolated figure who proclaims the end of the world, to no particular audience at all. The liberals' Jesus is an individual teacher who does not engage in give-and-take communication with others in ordinary social interaction. He utters individual sayings that apparently were heard only by individuals, who remembered them and then transmitted them to other individuals. This individualism is evident in Crossan's casting aside of previous reading of Jesus' proclamation of the kingdom of God against the background of the covenantal and prophetic traditions in which God was the true, transcendent ruler (king) of Israel and ultimately, of all history. As noted in Chapter 2, he opts rather for the kingdom that comes to the individual mystical philosopher in meditation on and personal intimacy with heavenly wisdom, as articulated by elite Hellenistic Jews such as Philo of Alexandria. It is as if no one had noticed that the pronoun "you" in Luke 17:21 is plural, so that the translation should be not "the kingdom of God is *within* you" but "the kingdom of God is *among* you" or *in the midst of* the group or the people.

Ironies abound in the various interpretations of Jesus, most of which assume and project modern individualism onto Jesus, while taking note of comparative or contextual material in which relations between leader and followers or movements are central. Crossan's and Allison's treatments are again illustrative of common scholarly assumptions and presentations. In Jesus' historical context of Roman Galilee and Judea, Crossan takes extensive note of popular prophets and popular messiahs and the movements they were leading. Yet in order to develop his governing paradigm of Jesus as teaching an unmediated relation of the individual and God, he projects the individual sage teaching a kingdom of God for the "child"-like individual.[4] In a "Detached Note" uncoordinated with his reassertion of the apocalyptic Jesus, Allison makes a list of nineteen common features of "millenarianism" from many different societies and historical circumstances.[5] If we look closely at the particular cases from which he abstracts the features, however, they were movements of resistance to modern European or American colonial invasion (or parallel movements in medieval Europe) produced by the response of large numbers of followers to a leader or leaders. These collective responses to the impact of imperial expansion catalyzed by a "charismatic" leader, however, do not lead Allison (or others) to an investigation of Jesus as anything beyond an isolated individual preacher of the themes of the apocalyptic scenario.[6]

Almost certainly, traditional Christological concerns also help determine the construction of Jesus as an individual unengaged in contingent relationships and conflicts. Jesus Christ is both *the revealer* whose words are the vehicles of the revelation of God and *the redeemer* who in self-sacrifice died on the cross for people's sins. According to the standard Christian theological scheme of Christian origins (from Judaism), moreover, Jesus was an individual revealer who delivered teaching to individual disciples who *after* his death and resurrection formed commu-

---

4. Crossan devoted Part II of *Historical Jesus* to extensive discussion of the various types of agitators, rebels, and leaders of movements active in Roman Palestine around the time of Jesus. In discussion of Jesus in Part III, however, he constructed an abstract typology of quadrants in a scheme that coordinates the difference between scribal and popular and the dichotomy of "apocalyptic" and "sapiential." As discussed in Chapters 2-5 above, the latter categories do not apply to leaders or movements. He uses statements from the diaspora Jewish elite as evidence for the popular sapiential quadrant/ type. But to date there is no extant evidence for the existence of a popular/peasant sage in Galilee or Judea at the time.

5. In *Jesus of Nazareth: Millenarian Prophet* (Minneapolis: Fortress, 1998), pp. 78-94.

6. This is a contrast to the fully relational exploration by John G. Gager, *Kingdom and Community: The Social World of Early Christianity* (Englewood Cliffs, NJ: Prentice-Hall, 1975), not long after many of the studies of millenarian movements were published in the 1950s and 1960s.

nities that eventually became the church. In this scheme, Jesus himself did not catalyze a movement during his "ministry." But there is no reason why Jesus cannot have been *the revealer* and *redeemer* while also having been engaged in interaction and conflict with other people in the concrete circumstances and particular social (political-economic-religious) forms of first-century Roman Palestine.

Perhaps the way to move beyond the limiting and distorting individualism that is imposed on Jesus is to consider that he can have become a significant historical figure only through interaction with and leadership of other people in a concrete historical situation. It may be helpful to consider how other historical figures became historically significant. We would surely not presume to understand Martin Luther King mainly on the basis of some of his statements taken out of the context of his sermons and speeches. We would consider whole sermons and speeches, and we would recognize that those sermons and speeches were delivered to church services and rallies in the civil rights movement. Those sermons and speeches, moreover, were inspiration for actions of smaller or larger groups of people who were challenging established laws and law-enforcement at considerable personal risk in resistance to oppressive political-economic conditions.

The civil rights movement, furthermore, emerged at a particular time in United States history when a number of discernible key factors somehow converged. At that particular juncture in U.S. history, other leaders of other, parallel movements also emerged. King himself emerged as the principal charismatic leader of one particular movement based in black churches in the South, organized by the Southern Christian Leadership Conference, as he built on and adapted the traditional role of a black preacher.

And to consider yet another key factor in how King became a significant historical figure in a particular historical context, he and other leaders of other movements arose out of and drew creatively upon a deep cultural-historical tradition of values, ideals, and previous resistance to oppression. That tradition included the story of the liberation from bondage in Egypt led by the prophet Moses, Jesus' own nonviolent leadership and martyrdom, the Declaration of Independence, and the emancipation declaration and Fourteenth Amendment to the U.S. Constitution. It may also be significant that the social role that King adapted into that of an inspirational civil rights leader was rooted in the same cultural tradition in which he and his movement were rooted. Finally, at a crucial point at which he more boldly confronted the established order economically as well as in its perpetuation of the war in Vietnam, King's assassination made him a revered martyr for the movement for justice that he had led.

Using Martin Luther King as an example, it is thus evident that to adequately understand how a figure becomes highly significant historically, it is necessary to consider several interrelated factors or aspects. (1) Fundamental is the particular historical situation in which s/he operated, along with the other historical players and historical forces in the situation and the major problems that the society was dealing with, in order to understand the historical crisis s/he faced and the need, opening, and possibilities for leadership. (2) Closely related is the cultural tradition of the people in the situation of crisis that might provide the values, ideals, and precedents for responding creatively to the problematic situation. (3) Certain personal circumstances, qualities, and qualifications may contribute to the person becoming an effective leader. (4) More important is the role of leadership already given in the cultural tradition and group/society in crisis that the potential followers assume and the leader adapts. And finally, as all of these factors come together, (5) there is the leaders' interaction with the people-in-crisis in leading a movement that makes a significant difference in the historical situation. Although it may not be a factor for most historically significant figures, the historical example of King also includes another factor: (6) a decisive confrontation of the leader with the dominant order that results in martyrdom in which the figure becomes powerful in death so that the leader's paradigmatic influence continues and perhaps expands.

Considering these interrelated aspects, we can devise a relational and contextual approach to the historical Jesus. We can thus attempt to understand how (1) in the particular historical conditions of Roman domination that had created a crisis for the Judean and Galilean people, (2) working out of Israelite cultural tradition in which those people were rooted, (3) the uprooted Galilean artisan Jesus of Nazareth emerged as a leader (4) by adapting the social role of a prophet like Moses and Elijah (and/or a popular king like the young David) (5) in interaction with Galilean villagers who responded by forming a movement of renewal of Israel that expanded rapidly after his crucifixion by the Romans, partly because (6) he had become a revered martyr whose cause was (believed) vindicated by God.

This multifactored historical investigation includes important relational and contextual factors that have often been underplayed or ignored when dealing with Jesus.[7] Any historical figure is significant historically only insofar as s/he interacted and resonated with other people in decisive ways in a particular historical situation. And almost by definition, a leader is someone who decisively influences (persuades, inspires, organizes) followers in a seriously problematic historical situation in such a way that they gain new perspective and/or take decisive action. (This is what Max Weber meant in his concept of the *charismatic* leader.) A historical figure such as Jesus, therefore, can only be approached through the results of his interaction with people who responded to him in decisive ways in their particular historical conditions (aspect 5). What the Gospels provide us with sources for is just this interaction and its effects. But this means that what we have access to through the Gospels is not Jesus as he was in himself (as a lone individual, as imagined by many Jesus interpreters) but Jesus-in-movement, Jesus in his interaction with and effects on the communities of those who responded.

Furthermore, both leader and followers deal with a historical crisis on the basis of a particular cultural tradition. Their cultural tradition de-

7. Because they operate with a standardized set of issues and concepts and without the more precise historical knowledge that has only recently become available, it has simply not occurred to many interpreters of Jesus to investigate, in more precise terms, the particular historical conditions in which Jesus acted (aspect 1) and to investigate, in more precise terms, the cultural tradition out of which he and his followers operated (aspect 2). The essentialist modern scholarly constructs operative in the field, such as "Judaism/Jewish," "Hellenistic," "apocalyptic," or "sapiential," tend to obscure particular circumstances and conflicts. Almost completely ignored have been the particular social forms of ancient Galilean and Judean society, that is, the multigenerational family and the village community, and the social form(s) of the relationship between Jesus and those who responded to him (that is, a popular prophet or messiah leading a movement), which would have been rooted in Israelite cultural tradition.

termines both the repertoire of ideas and manner of social interactions by which they will respond to the problems in their historical situation (aspect 2). In situations of cultural and political conflict, leader and followers adapt and create on the basis of their cultural tradition, often in interaction with an invasive alien culture and/or a dominant imperial regime. Leaders and followers, moreover, interact in adaptation of certain roles indicated or institutionalized in their cultural or political tradition. In some cases these are institutionalized offices, as with Abraham Lincoln acting in the office of President of the United States leading the Civil War to maintain the Union and, in the process, emancipating the slaves. In other cases the interaction of leader and followers takes shape more informally, by adapting certain leadership roles and prototypes of movements given in the cultural tradition, such as Martin Luther King's and his followers' adaptation of the black preacher role into that of civil rights leader (aspect 4). In the case of Jesus, there were some distinctively Israelite leadership roles that we know were current among the Galilean and Judean people from other, parallel movements. Of primary interest are the movements led by popular prophets informed by memory of Moses and Joshua or by popular messiahs informed by memory of the young David.

With an approach that incorporates investigation of these multiple aspects it may now be possible to bring together two heretofore largely separate lines of investigation. First, recent investigations have led to a more precise sense of the historical political-economic-religious context of Jesus' mission and movement in Roman Galilee and Judea. These investigations enable us to cut through the synthetic essentialist constructs that have been blocking the way toward more precise historical understanding of the fundamental division and dynamics between the Galilean and Judean people and their imperial and local rulers. This division regularly erupted into open conflict, including movements of resistance and renewal. This will be explored in Chapter 7. Second, what have usually been separate recent investigations have led to an appreciation of the Gospels as stories and speeches (rather than mere collections of fragments of "data"). These other investigations may lead us to use of the Gospels as more complex portrayals of a relational Jesus in interaction and conflict. This will be the subject of Chapter 8.

Largely unexplored in previous constructions of the historical Jesus are the leadership roles and distinctive forms of movements in Israelite culture that informed other movements contemporary with Jesus and his movement — roles that Jesus and his followers may have adapted. In Chapter 7 we cannot deal with those parallel movements without recognizing these roles and forms. We are looking for leadership roles and forms of movements that are attested in our sources for the historical situation in Roman Galilee and Judea, not modern scholarly constructs of individual revealers/teachers such as "eschatological/apocalyptic prophet" or "sage" (or "Jewish cynic sage"). The latter were not leadership roles attested in ancient Judean sources for Galilee and Judea at the time of Jesus.

The steps in Chapters 7 and 8 will prepare the way for a provisional attempt in Chapters 9 and 10 to move from the Gospel sources to the Jesus-in-movement that they portray, attempting to bring together the multiple aspects in a more complex, relational, and contextual sketch of the historical Jesus.

CHAPTER SEVEN

Renewal of Israel in Opposition to Imperial Rule

In the horrifying nightmare recounted in Daniel 7, the series of empires that dominated Judea appear as terrifying overwhelming predatory beasts that devour people and devastate their land. The crisis of imperial rule addressed by the visions in Daniel and Enoch texts came to a head when the Hellenistic emperor Antiochus Epiphanes invaded Jerusalem in 168 BCE to suppress the traditional Judean way of life. Several circles of scribes resisted, and a popular uprising of villagers led by Judas "the Maccabee" (hammer) managed to hold off the imperial armies through guerrilla warfare. The Hasmonean brothers who led "the Maccabean Revolt," however, soon set themselves up as the new high-priestly rulers. Several decades later, moreover, with an increasingly mercenary army, the Hasmonean high priests took to conquering the other areas of Palestine, setting up a regional empire of their own. Despite the resistance of the Pharisees and others, they successively took control of Idumea to the south, then Samaria to the north, where they destroyed the Samaritans' temple, and finally Galilee farther north (in 104 BCE). They required the Galileans to obey "the laws of the Judeans" (presumably laws about tithes, offerings, and other revenues due to the Temple and priesthood) if they wished to remain on their land (Josephus, *Ant.* 13.318-19). Thus, for at least a few generations, the Galileans and Samaritans lived under the same high-priestly rulers in the same capital, Jerusalem, as their fellow Israelites in Judea had for the previous centuries.

The Roman imperial conquest and repeatedly intrusive rule that began in 63 BCE must have come as a shock to the people at all levels.[1] The Roman warlord Pompey's invasion of the sacred inner precincts of the Temple shocked the scribes and Pharisees, along with the priests and ordinary Jerusalemites. In the countryside, as more critical recent classical historians are now explaining, Roman military conquests were intentionally and systematically brutal.[2] The Roman legions purposely terrorized subject peoples in the "shock and awe" devastation of villages and their land, slaughter or enslavement of the people, and public crucifixion of any who dared lead resistance. The Judean historian Josephus has several accounts of the periodic Roman devastation of districts of Galilee and Judea, including a massacre in Magdala a generation or so before Mary Magdalene, the destruction of Sepphoris (and some villages?) a few miles from Nazareth right around the time of Jesus' birth, and the devastation of Emmaus, on the road to which Luke locates Jesus' appearance to some of his disciples (*War* 1.180; 2.68-76; *Ant.* 17.288-295; Luke 24:13-27). Villagers in particular suffered repeated violence from Roman military actions to suppress the persistent resistance and periodic insurrection of the people. The Roman conquest of Palestine also brought escalated economic burdens to the people as well as death and destruction, as the Romans placed the conquered people under tribute. Based on their "census" of the territory and people, they fixed the tribute at 25 percent every second year (except sabbatical years, when the land was supposed to lie fallow).

To establish more rigorous control of Galilee and Judea, the Romans appointed the military strongman Herod as "King of the Judeans" in 40 BCE. After the three years it took him to beat down resistance of his subjects, he maintained tight, repressive control of the expanded territories

---

1. Fuller discussion of Roman conquest, imperial rule, and client rulers in Horsley, *Jesus and the Spiral of Violence: Popular Jewish Resistance in Roman Palestine* (San Francisco: Harper & Row, 1987; Minneapolis: Fortress, 1993), chap 2; *Jesus and Empire: The Kingdom of God and the New World Disorder* (Minneapolis: Fortress, 2003), ch. 1.

2. A good example is Susan P. Mattern, *Rome and the Enemy: Imperial Strategy and the Principate* (Berkeley: University of California Press, 1999).

that Rome placed under his rule until his death in 4 BCE. Herod, the emperor Augustus' favorite client king, built whole new cities named after the emperor, Caesarea and Sebaste (= Augustus), as well as several temples in honor of Caesar. In Jerusalem he undertook a massive reconstruction of the whole temple-mount, such that "Herod's Temple" became one of the great wonders of the Roman imperial world. Symbolizing the role of the rebuilt temple-complex in the imperial order, Herod placed a great golden eagle above the temple-gate. His massive building projects and lavish gifts to the imperial family and to Hellenistic cities, of course, placed considerable burdens on his subjects whom he taxed heavily to pay for them. As he lay dying, students of two leading scribal teachers cut down the Roman eagle in protest — and were tortured to death by Herod.[3] After he died Jerusalem erupted in protest, and widespread popular revolts erupted in Galilee and the trans-Jordan as well as in Judea.

The Roman Imperial (Dis)Order in Judea and Galilee

After their brutal reconquest, the Romans placed Galilee under Herod's son Antipas. Throughout Jesus' lifetime Galileans were under Antipas' rule, not the direct jurisdiction of Jerusalem. The Romans placed Judea (and Samaria) under the control of the high-priestly aristocracy of the four families that Herod had previously installed in office, under the oversight of a Roman governor located in the new city of Caesarea on the coast. In Galilee Herod Antipas built two new capital cities within his first twenty years of rule, again increasing the tax-burden of his subjects. In Jerusalem the high-priestly families built themselves increasingly lavish palaces and, according to the historian Josephus, became ever more predatory on the Judean villagers.

These principal events and figures involved in Roman imperial rule of Judea, Samaria, and Galilee illustrate the basic divide between rulers and ruled mentioned briefly in Chapter 5.[4] As the fundamental units of

3. Closer analysis of Josephus' accounts in Horsley, *Jesus and the Spiral of Violence*, pp. 71-77.

4. On the basic divide in Roman Galilee and Judea between the rulers and the peo-

production in a traditional agrarian society, village families were also the economic base from which the rulers derived their revenues, in the form of tribute, taxes, tithes, and offerings. Precisely those parallel forms of revenues indicate that under Roman rule the people of Galilee and Judea had sometimes two layers and sometimes effectively three layers of rulers and demands on their produce. The increased economic pressure, along with the effects of periodic Roman reconquest, was surely a major factor in the social unrest and regular resistance among the Galilean and Judean people. Families that could no longer feed themselves after yielding up tribute, taxes, and tithes from the piles of grain on their threshing floors had to borrow, and they fell ever more deeply into debt. Josephus indicates that Herod had to offer tax relief lest he destroy his economic base in the productive peasantry — the proverbial geese that keep laying what become the golden eggs of the wealthy and powerful ruling families. As families fell into hunger and debt, the village communities that comprised the basic social form of any agrarian society would have begun to disintegrate, unable to support one another. Such are the conditions from which popular movements regularly originate.

While there was no middle class in ancient societies, in Judea the scribes and Pharisees were "in the middle" between the rulers and the villagers. They were important for the operation of the temple-state in Jerusalem as advisors to high priests, as those who cultivated the laws and other Judean cultural traditions (Sirach 38:24–39:4).[5] While they

---

ple, the basic social forms, and the political-economic dynamics, see further Horsley, *Sociology and the Jesus Movement* (New York: Crossroad, 1989).

5. Anthony Saldarini, *Pharisees, Scribes, and Sadducees* (Wilmington, DE: Glazier, 1988), explains, on the basis of the historical sociology of Gerhard Lenski, that the scribes and Pharisees were the legal-intellectual retainers of the Jerusalem temple-state. For evidence from and analysis of the scribes in Judean texts such as the book of Sirach, see Horsley, *Scribes, Visionaries, and the Politics of Second Temple Judea* (Louisville: Westminster John Knox, 2007), esp. chs. 3 and 4. This professional role of scribes in cultivating the Judean cultural repertoire may be what the Judean historian Josephus is attempting to convey by presenting the Pharisees, Sadducees, and Essenes as similar to the Greek "philosophies" (*War* 2.119, 162-65; *Ant.* 18:11-22). Modern scholars, however, have somewhat misleadingly labeled them as the "sects" of Judaism, projecting an analogy to the "sects" that emerged during the Protestant Reformation as smaller groups separate from the established "church(es)" in German territories or England.

were more or less dependent economically on the Jerusalem high-priestly rulers, some of the scribes and Pharisees often sympathized with the people and opposed the high-priestly rulers, especially when they collaborated too closely with the Roman imperial rulers. As the Jerusalem scribe Jesus ben Sira also mentions (38:27-32; see Chapter 5 above) among the ordinary people of Jerusalem were artisans of various kinds who served the needs of the Temple and the desires of the wealthy aristocracy. Although they too were economically dependent on the Temple and aristocracy, they regularly protested the practices of the rulers.

The historian Josephus recounts how social unrest periodically erupted and how it escalated steadily in the middle of the first century CE. He tells of protests usually mounted by the ordinary people of Jerusalem or the villagers, but mentions also occasionally protests by scribal groups. Most striking is that the mission of Jesus is framed by the widespread revolts against the Roman and Jerusalem rulers in 4 BCE and the great revolt of 66-70 CE. Jesus and his movement emerged in just this historical context. Thus a survey of both the scribal texts and protests and the popular movements of resistance and renewal may help elucidate Jesus' mission, the role(s) he adapted, and the movement that focused on him.[6]

Hopes, Protests, and Movements
for Renewal of Israel in Scribal Circles

While the primary concern of apocalyptic texts was evidently explanation of how the crisis under imperial rule had developed and reassurance that it would (soon) be resolved by the ultimate governance of history by the Most High, they do articulate a hope for the restoration of Judean society.[7] As noted in Chapter 5 above, however briefly at the end of the historical visions-and-interpretations in Daniel 7 and 10–12, the visionaries offer the confident hope for the restoration of the now-

6. For more systematic investigation and analysis of these conflicts, with references, see Horsley, *Jesus and the Spiral of Violence*, chs. 2, 3, 4.

7. For more extensive analysis and discussion of both the apocalyptic texts and scribal movements of protest, see Horsley, *Revolt of the Scribes: Resistance and Apocalyptic Origins* (Minneapolis: Fortress, 2010).

persecuted people as the counterpart of God's termination of imperial rule. "The one like a son of man" who is given dominion in Daniel 7 is explained as "the people of the holy ones of the Most High." After Antiochus Epiphanes "shall come to his end," Michael, the great protector of the Judean people, shall arise in the divine court, and the people will be delivered. This restoration of the people includes the resurrection of some (the righteous) to everlasting life and others (presumably those who abandoned the covenant with God) to everlasting contempt, and the vindication of the wise scribes who had been martyred in the course of resisting the imperial persecution (12:1-3).

The contemporary early "Enoch" texts, the Animal Vision and the Ten-Week Vision, look for a broader, almost universal renewal of all peoples under a restored divine governance of a "new heaven." The decisive event leading to the broader renewal is the restoration of the Judean people/Israel. In the Animal Vision, the Lord of the sheep brings "a new house, larger and higher than the first one" where all of the sheep, their eyes now opened, are gathered (*1 Enoch* 90:28-36). The house, however, has no tower, the previous tower (the second Temple) having had "polluted bread on its table" (89:73). The restored people (of Judea/Israel) is clearly the focus of the resolution to the crisis under oppressive imperial rule. The Ten-Week Vision also looks for "the house of the kingdom of the Great One" to be built in the greatness of its glory (again the people of God, not the Temple) in the eighth week, but gives more attention to the revelation of the justice of the Torah to all peoples under the new heaven of divine governance in the ninth and tenth weeks (*1 Enoch* 91:12-17).

The expression of similar hope for and confidence in the restoration of Israel continued into early Roman rule. Some scribal circle must be responsible for the "updating" of the *Testament of Moses,* another vision-and-interpretation (the earlier version of which had addressed the persecution by Antiochus Epiphanes). The closing prophetic oracle (ch. 10) articulates the hope for God's judgment of the empire and restoration of the people in more fantastic terms, including the vindication of the whole people that had pertained more specifically to the martyred sages in Daniel 12:3.

Hope for and confidence in the future restoration of Israel receive more elaborate shape in the non-apocalyptic Psalms of Solomon 17, composed under Roman rule, probably during or just following the reign of Herod the Great. This text is usually cited as *the* statement of the Jewish expectation of "the Messiah, Son of David," and readers miss the concrete restoration of Israel which the anointed son of David is expected to accomplish as God's agent. As the counterpart of destroying the imperial rulers, he will "gather a holy people, . . . establish justice for the tribes . . . and distribute them on the land according to their tribes. . . . He will purge Jerusalem," and establish justice among the people so that none will be oppressed (17:26-32, 41). This is clearly a vision of scribes, who are oriented toward Jerusalem and who conceive of the anointed one in scribal terms (acting primarily in the words of his mouth). In comparison with Daniel 12:1-3, where the concern is primarily for vindication of the martyred scribes, the scope here includes all of the people, according to the traditional ideal of the twelve tribes on their land.

Since the discovery of the Dead Sea Scrolls, we have abundant evidence for the scribal-priestly group that withdrew into the wilderness at Qumran in protest evidently against the imperial behavior of the new Hasmonean high priesthood. They understood their movement as a new exodus and the foundation of a renewed Mosaic covenant, as exemplified and articulated in their Community Rule, which takes the traditional form of a covenant and includes instructions for a regular covenant-renewal ceremony. That their covenantal community was also a renewed Israel is indicated in the council of twelve members, and since it was a priestly community it also had three priests. The role of the Righteous Teacher as the leader-founder of the community is evidently patterned after the role of Moses, the founding prophet of Israel. Some of the documents of the community at Qumran mention the "anointed ones" of Aaron and Israel. But they have no formative roles for the covenantal community; they have only an evidently ritual role in the ceremonial meals of the more formal future fulfillment of the renewed Israel.

Another action of a circle of scribes rooted in their commitment to the Mosaic covenant, but in direct confrontation with the Roman imperial order, in contrast to the withdrawal to Qumran, was the movement of resistance to payment of the tribute to Rome. This was mounted by what Josephus calls "the fourth philosophy," led by the scribal teacher Judas of Gamala (east of Galilee in Gaulanitis) and the Pharisee Saddok. According to Josephus' account, they agreed basically with the Pharisees, except that they were ready to take action on the basis of their conviction that Israel owed exclusive loyalty to God as its ruler. Their action in resistance to the tribute is thus evidently based on the first and second commandments (no other gods, and not bowing down and serving, with tribute and taxes, the gods symbolized in "idols"). Theirs was an initiative of the renewal of Israel in concrete political-economic action to resist the imperial rule of Caesar, who claimed the people's service in economic form.[8]

How Can We Know about Popular Movements?

Another of the anachronistic synthetic concepts that we have been projecting onto Galilean and Judean society at the time of Jesus is "the Bible." Scholars are presumably aware that neither the Hebrew Bible nor the New Testament had yet been delimited and "canonized" as the recognized "Scripture" of the distinct religions of "Judaism" and "Christianity." They nevertheless apply the terms "Bible" and "biblical history" and "Scripture" loosely to first-century texts and history and texts, assuming for example that they can use books of the Hebrew Bible (whose texts have been "established" by modern text-critics) as direct sources for social-religious life and expectations of "the Jews" in Roman Palestine. It has been a standard assumption that "the Jews" were a "people of the Book," with widespread literacy and readily available scrolls of the Scriptures ("the Law and the Prophets"). Recent research on orality and literacy in antiquity (including Judea and Galilee) and recent research on the scrolls of books later included in the Hebrew Bible that were found among the Dead Sea Scrolls, however, have shown the old assumption to be unfounded. Text critic Eugene Ulrich has explained that the manuscripts of books such as Genesis or Deuteronomy or Isaiah

---

8. For earlier analysis of the Fourth Philosophy, see Richard Horsley with John Hanson, *Bandits, Prophets, and Messiahs* (Minneapolis: Winston, 1985), pp. 190-200; and Horsley, *Jesus and the Spiral of Violence*, pp. 77-89.

found among the Dead Sea Scrolls represent two or three different versions of these texts, all of which were still developing, and not yet stable in their wording.[9] Because of specialization in biblical studies, however, few interpreters of Jesus have yet taken these challenging recent researches into account.

Extensive research has now confirmed that literacy in Roman Palestine was limited to around 3 percent of the people, i.e., basically to scribal circles.[10] Communication among Galileans and Judeans was predominantly oral. Writing simply was not needed and not used for most interactions and transactions. More recently we have become aware that the scribes who made written copies of books of Torah or of prophetic oracles learned and cultivated them mainly by oral recitation. Scribes could apparently recite a passage of "scripture" from memory, as appropriate, without consulting ("reading") a written text. Scrolls of scriptural books were extremely expensive and cumbersome, and not readily available. Only scribes could read them anyhow, and they had to be already familiar with a given text in order to decipher/decode the words on the scroll, which had no spaces in between and no punctuation. Ordinary people would have known about the existence of texts or Torah or prophets that existed in writing. But they would have had no direct contact with them. The portrayal of Jesus opening a scroll of Isaiah and "reading" the text is probably a projection back to Jesus by the Gospel of Luke of a recitation of scripture from an open scroll in the meeting house of a diaspora Jewish congregation.[11]

That Galilean and Samaritan and Judean villagers did not have direct contact with, hence probably no direct knowledge of written texts of the books that were later included in the Hebrew Bible, however, does

9. See particularly Eugene Ulrich, *The Dead Sea Scrolls and the Origins of the Bible* (Grand Rapids: Eerdmans, 1999), esp. pp. 11, 14, 40-41, 91-92, 102.

10. Extensively researched and presented by Catherine Hezser, *Jewish Literacy in Roman Palestine,* Texte und Studien zum antiken Judentum (Tübingen: Mohr Siebeck, 2001).

11. For the implications of recent research on these matters, see Richard A. Horsley with Jonathan A. Draper, *Whoever Hears You Hears Me: Prophets, Performance, and Tradition in Q* (Harrisburg, PA: Trinity Press International, 1999), ch. 6; and Richard A. Horsley, *Scribes, Visionaries, and the Politics of Second Temple Judea* (Louisville: Westminster John Knox, 2007).

not mean they were ignorant of Israelite tradition. On the contrary, like other peoples, the ordinary people at the time of Jesus cultivated the traditions that were special to them orally in their village communities. Anthropologists make a distinction between the "great tradition" and the "little tradition" in many societies. The "great tradition" is the official version of the people's cultural heritage, some of which may have been written down, and is cultivated by a cultural elite, often as a way of legitimating the power and privilege of a ruling elite. The "little tradition" is the popular version of the society's cultural heritage cultivated by the people themselves orally, partly as the customs and rules that guide local interaction in the village communities. The popular tradition is often taken up into the official tradition, perhaps involving some cooptation. This can be seen, for example, in the incorporation and editing of stories of Elijah and Elisha in 1 Kings 17–21 and 2 Kings 1–9. And rulers press the great tradition on the people as the official version of the (supposedly) common cultural heritage.[12]

Because ordinary people, who are usually nonliterate, do not leave written sources for their life and views, we usually have no evidence except the often-hostile reports of the literate elite. And those reports often come when the people disrupt the established order. The Judean historian Josephus provides just such hostile accounts of many popular protests and movements among the Galilean, Samaritan, and Judean villagers around the time of Jesus. It is necessary to read critically through his hostility. By doing so we not only have access to the popular movements but also to the Israelite popular tradition in which they were rooted and whose currency they attest in the society at the time of Jesus.

Popular Movements of the Renewal of Israel Against the Rulers

Prior to consideration of the many popular movements of resistance and renewal in early Roman Palestine, we look briefly at two popular protests

---

12. Fuller discussion in Horsley (with Draper), *Whoever Hears You Hears Me*, ch. 5; and Horsley, *Hearing the Whole Story: The Politics of Plot in Mark's Gospel* (Louisville: Westminster John Knox, 2001), pp. 156-61.

that indicate how the most foundational events and patterns in Israelite tradition set up conflict and confrontation with Roman imperial rule. Passover was the annual celebration of the people's liberation from bondage under a foreign imperial rule in Egypt. Centuries earlier, however, what had been observed as a celebration of families in their village communities was centralized in the Temple, as a way of bringing more control and revenue into the hands of the Jerusalem rulers. The imposition of direct Roman rule in Judea, however, brought the celebration of the people's liberation in the weeklong Passover festival into direct juxtaposition with the new form of imperial domination. Indeed the Passover celebration in Herod's Temple became a flashpoint for potential protest against Roman domination. In a typical imperial show of force intended for its repressive effect, the Roman governors made a practice of bringing a company of soldiers into Jerusalem and posting them "on the porticoes of the Temple so as to quell any uprising that might occur" (*Ant.* 20.106). At one Passover in mid-first century a lewd gesture by a soldier to the crowd below touched off a vigorous protest. The governor responded by sending his military forces into the Temple courtyard against the protesters, which panicked the crowd into a stampede in which many were crushed to death.[13]

Another popular protest illustrates not only how Roman imperial rule was unacceptable according to the Mosaic covenant, but how its enforcement forced the people to violate the covenant commandments. It also illustrates the remarkable ability of villagers to organize collective action. What touched off the widespread protest of Galilean peasants was the Roman army marching through their land on an expedition to install a statue of the emperor Gaius (Caligula) in the Jerusalem Temple, in blatant violation of the commandment against bowing down to idols/ images representing (other) gods. But of course the Roman demand of tribute was already a standing violation of the first two commandments, which forced the people into violation year after year. In response to Gaius' order, Galilee villagers organized what was a widespread and sustained peasant strike (Josephus, *Ant.* 18.261-84). As Roman legions ad-

13. Fuller discussion of this incident in Horsley, *Jesus and the Spiral of Violence*, pp. 34-35.

vanced through Galilee the peasants formed mass protests, and to back up their demands refused to plant seed in the fields. That is, they were using about the only leverage they had, setting up a situation at harvest time in which there would be no crops from which the Romans could take their tribute. They were prepared to go hungry in order to stop yet another Roman encroachment on their lives.[14]

Right around the time of Jesus there were many (other) popular movements of resistance to the rulers and renewal of Israel, which took one or another of two forms distinctive to Israelite tradition. The popular revolts in Galilee, Judea, and the trans-Jordan following the death of Herod in 4 BCE all took the same social form. According to Josephus' horrified account (*Ant.* 17.271-81), these movements all acclaimed their leader as "king": in Galilee Judas, son of the brigand-chief Hezekiah, a man of great strength; across the Jordan Simon, another fellow of great size and strength; and in Judea a shepherd named Athronges, again of great stature and strength. In labeling the leaders "kings," Josephus is using a Greek term intelligible to his Hellenistic readers. That the participants in these movements "acclaimed" their leader as "king," however, is directly reminiscent of the stories of how first the tribe of Judah and then the elders of all Israel "anointed" (literally, "messiahed") David as their chieftain to lead them in resistance to the Philistines — stories that would have been well known in the popular Israelite tradition cultivated among villagers as well as included in the (written) text of 2 Samuel. According to the stories in 1 Samuel, moreover, the young David who was thus "messiahed" had been a shepherd-turned-warrior and a brigand-chief. It seems that what lies behind Josephus' accounts are several popular messianic movements.[15]

After the tyrannical oppressive rule of Herod, who had been installed by the Romans as "King of the Judeans," the people were eager to have a king from among their own ranks who would lead them in throwing off the yoke of Roman rule, just as David had led their ancestors in beating back the Philistines. Far from looking to aristocratic families for leader-

14. Fuller discussion in Horsley, *Jesus and the Spiral of Violence*, pp. 110-16.

15. More extensive analysis of Josephus' accounts and the roots of these movements in Israelite tradition in Horsley with Hanson, *Bandits, Prophets, and Messiahs*, ch. 3.

ship, the people focused on charismatic figures of humble origins. Hezekiah had been a popular brigand-chieftain in Galilee whom the young military strongman Herod had killed, evoking an outcry among the people. So it is very likely that a son of such a popular hero could have quickly emerged as the acclaimed leader of the uprising in Galilee. It is also likely either that the people would have looked to a figure of great stature and strength as their leader in revolt, or that these charismatic "new Davids" would have quickly gained an aura of physical prowess as warriors and of legendary origin as shepherds.

All of these movements were of considerable size and were well organized. In Galilee and the trans-Jordan they attacked the Herodian palaces/fortresses and took back the goods that had been seized and stored there. In Judea, Athronges and his people attacked both Roman and Herodian troops and raided Roman baggage trains. Moreover, these movements succeeded in establishing the people's independence and self-governance for at least a short time before the Romans could reconquer their areas. The movement led by Athronges maintained the people's independence for three years in northwestern Judea. More than revolts, these were movements of deliverance and renewal of the people led by popularly acclaimed (anointed) kings. These were *popular* "messiahs," moreover, in contrast to the *imperial* king exemplified by Solomon, the son of David, legitimated in the promise to David in 2 Samuel 7, and celebrated in Psalms 2 and 110.

Again seventy years later amidst the great revolt of 66-70 against the Romans, Herodians, and high-priestly rulers, another popular messianic movement emerged, on a yet wider scale. Again according to Josephus' account, Simon bar Giora and his movement exhibited several features reminiscent of the prototypical movement led by the young David. Simon gathered a following in the hill country of Judea, "proclaiming freedom of (debt-)slaves and reward for the free" (*War* 2.652-53; 4.507-13). He established a base at Hebron, where David had first been "messiahed" king (4:529-34). Once he and his followers took over much of the city of Jerusalem, they were the principal fighting force in resistance to the Roman siege. When the Romans finally conquered Jerusalem, they took Simon prisoner and formally executed him in a great triumphal procession in Rome as "the king of the Judeans" (7:29-31, 36, 13-55). Again, with such a social program of liberation for debt-slaves and freedom from Roman rule, the popular messianic movement led by Simon bar Giora was a renewal of the people as well as a revolt.[16] While the popular messianic tradition of the young David may have lain dormant for centuries (we have no record), popular messianic movements became prominent as one of the principal social forms of renewal of the people in early Roman times.

Shortly after the mission of Jesus, at mid-first century, a number of other popular movements arose that were all led by prophets.[17] A few years after Jesus' mission, the leader of a movement in Samaria urged his followers up the slopes of Mount Gerizim, the most sacred mountain, where they were to find the holy vessels of the ancient tabernacle on top of the mountain where Moses had buried them (*Ant.* 18.86-87). A decade later, around 45 CE, there was a similar movement (also mentioned in Acts 5:36, but mistakenly dated forty years earlier). A prophet named Theudas "persuaded most of the common people to take their possessions and follow him to the Jordan River, where at his command the river would be divided and allow them an easy crossing" (*Ant.* 20.97-98). Another decade later, in 55 or 56 CE, in a movement that Acts 21:38 confuses with the terrorist scribal *Sicarii* ("Dagger-Men"), a prophet arriving at Jerusalem from Egypt "led the mass of the common people to go to the Mount of Olives, just opposite the city. He said that at his command the walls of Jerusalem would fall down" and they could then make an entry into the city (*Ant.* 20.169-71). That these movements involved "the majority of the masses" or "30,000 people," while probably exaggerations, indicates that they were large movements involving a widespread longing of villagers at the time for liberation and renewal. Worried that these clearly nonviolent movements were serious threats to the imperial order, the Roman governors at the time, Pontius Pilate, Fadus, and Felix, quickly sent out their military. In their usual brutality, they killed hundreds of the participants, took other hundreds prisoner (to be sold into

16. Sixty years later the final Judean revolt against Roman rule was led by Bar Kokhba, whom the revered rabbi Akiba acclaimed as "the king, the messiah" (*y. Ta'an.* 4.8 [68d 48-51]).

17. More extensive analysis of Josephus' accounts and the roots of these movements in Israelite tradition in Horsley with Hanson, *Bandits, Prophets, and Messiahs,* ch. 4.

slavery?), and executed the "ringleaders." In the case of the prophet Theudas, they cut off his head and carried it into Jerusalem.

Judging from Josephus' more general summary accounts there must have been several other such movements at mid-century. His hostile summary statements that these "impostors and demagogues" led the people out into the wilderness where they would display unmistakable "signs and wonders" of God's imminent liberation (*War* 2.259; *Ant.* 20.168) have misled modern scholars into labeling the leaders as "sign prophets." Yet as Josephus knew, "signs and wonders" were standard symbols for the exodus and wilderness stories. So those symbols and the rest of his summaries, which say the prophets worked under "divine inspiration," provoking "revolutionary actions by the masses acting like madmen" to march "into the wilderness" where they would experience "imminent liberation" — along with his accounts of the three particular prophets and their movements — are telling indications of what these movements were about. All of these movements were clearly reminiscences or reenactments of earlier Israelite movements led by a prophet, such as the exodus from bondage, the wilderness march, and the entry into the land (e.g., "the battle of Jericho") led by Moses and Joshua, with echoes of Elijah and his protégé Elisha in the wilderness and crossing the Jordan as well. The memories of God's great foundational acts of deliverance and formation of the people through Moses and Joshua and the new liberation and renewal of the people through Elijah and "the children of the prophets" were very much alive at the time. These memories at the core of Israelite popular tradition provided the pattern or prototype for these movements focused on God's new acts of deliverance and renewal. That the prophets and their followers struck the wealthy aristocrat Josephus as "inspired" and "acting like madmen" suggests that they were indeed acting in the power of an energizing collective spirit, just as Elijah and "the children of the prophets" were acting in the power of the spirit of Yahweh. And that the followers of Theudas took their possessions with them indicates that they were not going out to the wilderness simply for a one-day picnic or demonstration.

The similar form and purpose of all these movements, along with their differences in particularities, suggest a common pattern that was very much alive in Israelite culture at the time of Jesus, clearly rooted in the collective memory of the ancient formative prophetic movements led by Moses, Joshua, or Deborah (also known as a prophet, Judg. 5), or Elijah. These were not simply prophets who delivered oracles against the kings and their officers for exploiting the people, such as Amos or Isaiah or Jeremiah. There were still (or again) prophets of this type in first-century Judea, as illustrated by that other peasant prophet named Jesus, son of Hananiah, who pronounced oracles of doom on the city of Jerusalem in the years prior to and during the eruption of the great revolt. Theudas, the Samaritan, and the prophet returned from Egypt were rather prophets who led movements of deliverance and formation or renewal of the people, like Moses, Joshua, Deborah, and Elijah.

The popular prophetic movements and the popular messianic movements thus offer examples not only of movements among the people pursuing independence from imperial rule and renewal of Israelite society in justice under the direct rule of its God. They also indicate the currency, indeed prominence, among the people of Israelite heritage at the time, of cultural patterns that included role-models that leaders could adapt and followers respond to, or perhaps project onto a leader. Moreover, the two roles of popular messiah and popular prophet leading a movement, along with that of an oracular prophet, are the only three roles at the popular level that we have evidence for. While we know about scribal teachers, and even one who led a movement of scribes and priests as the Righteous Teacher at Qumran, we have no evidence for the role of a sage at the popular level, much less a popular sapiential teacher who would have catalyzed a movement of renewal. The evidence offered for the supposed role of a "holy man," like the later rabbinized rainmaker Honi the Circle Drawer and Hanina ben Dosa, has been sharply criticized and discounted.[18] The fact that Jesus of Nazareth is extensively represented as a prophet like Moses and Elijah in the Gospels and that he is also, with some reservations, identified as an/the anointed one in the Gospels and bears the name Jesus Christ (Messiah) in Paul's letters suggests critical investigation of whether the historical Jesus and his movement(s) were adapting one or both of these roles, while pursuing the renewal of Israel in resistance to the rulers.

18. See esp. John P. Meier, *A Marginal Jew: Rethinking the Historical Jesus,* vol. 2: *Mentor, Message, and Miracles* (New York: Doubleday, 1994), pp. 581-88.

CHAPTER EIGHT

The Gospel Sources for Jesus' Mission

⎯⎯⎯⎯⟋⟍⎯⎯⎯⎯

O ne of the most basic responsibilities of historians is to critically assess the character of their sources, as noted in Chapter 6. The principal sources for the historical Jesus are the Gospels. Yet, for various reasons, including deeply ingrained habits of reading the Bible, the Gospels were taken as mere containers of Jesus' sayings and other bits and pieces of "data" that could be culled out of them for scholars to use in their reconstructions.

Well before the current wave of investigation of the historical Jesus gained momentum, however, other New Testament scholars were (re-) discovering the literary integrity of the Gospels as whole stories about Jesus' mission in interactive speech and action. Perhaps most important was the recognition that the Gospels were sustained narratives comprised of many episodes that were components of the developing story and intelligible only in the broader context of the whole story.[1] The Gospels, moreover, were not just one episode after another, but were stories

1. Influential early treatments were Werner H. Kelber, *Mark's Story of Jesus* (Philadelphia: Fortress, 1979); David Rhoads and Donald Michie, *Mark as Story: An Introduction to the Narrative of a Gospel* (Philadelphia: Fortress, 1982); Jack Dean Kingsbury, *Matthew as Story* (Philadelphia: Fortress, 1984). Critical review of literary critical readings of the whole Gospel stories in Stephen D. Moore, *Literary Criticism and the Gospels: The Theoretical Challenge* (New Haven: Yale University Press, 1989).

with overall plots, in which earlier episodes and events both set up and led to subsequent episodes and events.

In the flush of discovery a generation ago, Gospel interpreters took many cues from criticism of modern narrative fiction in university departments of literary studies. The Gospels were read like modern novels or short stories, with (implied) authors, narrators, and implied readers. Interpreters looked for suspenseful plots and character development.

The Gospels, however, are different from modern novellas in significant ways. The plots of the Gospels are not linear, and are not full of suspense. Gospel stories have clear implications of how they will come out, in narratives the plots of which are known before they are read or heard. The characters are types, even stereotypes, playing important roles but not undergoing "character development." The Gospel stories, moreover, are not comparable to modern fiction insofar as they purpose to be historical stories, indeed are filled with claims that they are the fulfillment of history. To be understood they therefore must be read in the historical context in which they are set.[2] It may thus be helpful to begin with some of the fundamental questions asked of stories in *Literature 101:* the stories' (historical) setting, the principal characters, and the overall plot. As the first step in approaching the historical Jesus it is necessary to take the Gospel stories whole, to appreciate their overall portrayal of Jesus' mission in interaction with followers and the rulers of the people in the circumstances of the historical setting. Only after getting clarity on the sources will it then be possible to assess their portrayals in the historical context as known from other sources and to compare the portrayals in the different Gospels.

In order to make the project manageable and simplify the presentation we will focus on what are, by a considerable consensus, the earliest Gospel sources, the Gospel of Mark and the "source" ("Q," short for *Quelle*) of the Jesus-speeches that are parallel in Matthew and Luke.

---

2. An attempt to do this is Richard Horsley, *Hearing the Whole Story: The Politics of Plot in Mark's Gospel* (Louisville: Westminster John Knox, 2001).

The Gospel of Mark

Mark's story of Jesus is situated in Roman Palestine. For much of the story, the action takes place in Galilee, the northernmost area of Israelite heritage that had been separate under Jerusalem rule about a hundred years before Jesus and during his lifetime had been placed by the Romans under the control of Antipas, son of Herod the Great. Jesus also moves across the frontier to other areas. Mark has Jesus working mainly in Galilean and other villages, and never venturing into the capital cities. As the story moves toward the climactic events, however, Jesus moves through Judea and up to Jerusalem, where his sustained confrontation with the high-priestly rulers takes place in the Temple. In a distinctive twist, the disciples are directed back to Galilee at the end, where the raised Jesus has gone to meet them.

As in most ancient stories, the characters are stereotyped, but those we would expect in the settings. In the simple narrative style of most episodes there are only two or at most three main characters. The disciples are called and commissioned as associates of Jesus from the start. In the village scenes, Jesus interacts with people who have illness and their supporters and onlookers. The scribes or Pharisees who have come down from Jerusalem dispute Jesus' actions. Unclean spirits and Satan play an occasional role in the first half of the story, and then disappear. Women play an increasingly prominent role as the story progresses. When Jesus goes up to Jerusalem for the Passover festival, the high priests, elders, and leading scribes take the leading roles in opposition to Jesus, as we would expect, since the high-priestly aristocracy had been placed in control of Judea under the oversight of a Roman governor after the death of Herod. Pontius Pilate enters the story only at the end, as the Roman governor who has the power of execution. God, Jesus' "Father," and Caesar are important in the story, but "off-stage."

The recognition of the Gospel of Mark as a sustained story did not lead directly to clarity about the Gospel's plot.[3] Presumably the plot of a story is integrally tied up with the dominant conflict as earlier events

---

3. Fuller analysis and discussion in Horsley, *Hearing the Whole Story*, ch. 4 and esp. ch. 5.

lead to the climactic events. Mark's story, however, has several interrelated conflicts. Most striking to many modern individualistic readers who still take the Gospel as a story primarily about personal faith is the conflict that develops in the course of the story between Jesus and his disciples. After Jesus calls disciples, appoints the Twelve, and commissions them to extend his own mission, they begin to be afraid, and seriously to misunderstand his mission. Finally as he is arrested, tried, and crucified, the disciples abandon, betray, and deny him. Many interpreters used their newly honed skills in literary criticism to reinforce the standard modern Christian understanding of Mark as about discipleship, focused on the disciples as the model of the struggle to remain faithful to their Lord.

In a story such as Mark's Gospel with several interrelated conflicts running through the narrative, it is necessary to distinguish the dominant conflict and plot from the secondary conflicts. The key is surely to be found in the climax of the story. Yes, the disciples do abandon, betray, and deny Jesus, but the dominant conflict once Jesus goes into Jerusalem is between Jesus and the Jerusalem and Roman rulers. Jesus confronts them in one episode of criticism and condemnation after another, in response to which the High Priests, elders, and scribes form a plot to arrest Jesus and have him killed. While the narrative of the disciples' betrayal, denial, and abandonment is interwoven with the arrest, trial, and crucifixion of Jesus, the focus is clearly on the conflict between Jesus and the Jerusalem and Roman rulers.

The same dominant conflict, however, runs throughout the Gospel as it builds up to the confrontation and climactic events in Jerusalem, even though the episodes earlier in the story do not directly or explicitly involve the rulers themselves. In his first exorcism, the people recognize that he "teaches with authority/power," unlike the scribes (in/from Jerusalem; 1:22-28). The scribes and Pharisees, who "come down from Jerusalem," object that he is arrogating to himself the prerogatives of the Temple and priesthood (2:1-12). After several such episodes, the Pharisees and Herodians plot how to destroy him, and accuse him of working in cahoots with Satan (3:6, 22). The story proceeds with no suspense, as Jesus himself announces three times that he "will be handed over to the High Priests and scribes, and they will condemn him to death; then hand him over to the nations . . . who will kill him; and then he will rise again" (8:31; 9:31; 10:33-34). Holding the dominant plot together at the beginning and end of the story are such themes as the conflict over who has "authority (power)," Jesus or the "authorities" (1:22-28; 11:27-33), and the scribes' and later the High Priests' charge of blasphemy, for which they condemn him to death (2:1-12; 14:61-64). As we know by comparison with the other Gospels, Mark seems to downplay the resurrection by having merely an empty tomb in the last episode (16:1-8). The latter, however, forms part of the Gospel's distinctive "open" ending, in which the disciples — and the readers — are directed to go (back) to Galilee where Jesus began his mission and where he has gone ahead expecting to meet them there (14:28; 16:7).

To see how Mark portrays Jesus we look further at the "substance" of the plot, at the center of which is the dominant conflict of Jesus with the rulers. In episode after episode and in a number of interrelated ways, Mark's story portrays Jesus as a prophet engaged in a renewal of Israel in opposition to and by the Jerusalem and Roman rulers of the people. At the outset of the story, John the Baptist steps forward as a prophet crying in the wilderness to prepare the way of the Lord (1:2-8). The "way of the Lord" is the new exodus that Jesus is about to lead, just as Moses had led the liberation from bondage in Egypt. As "the messenger of the covenant," moreover, John is enacting a renewal of the Mosaic covenant in his baptism of repentance. The baptism with Holy Spirit that Jesus will perform is the divine presence that will empower the new exodus and covenant, which is the renewal of the people of Israel. As the prophet of renewal, Jesus undergoes forty days' testing in the wilderness, just as Elijah had done in his preparation for leading the renewal of Israel, and as Moses had been tested in the wilderness before being sent to lead the exodus (1:12-13).

Jesus' call of the first disciples (1:16-20) then evokes memories of Elijah's call of Elisha and the bands of prophets with which Elijah was associated and the twelve stones of the altar that he built (1 Kings 18–19). When Jesus then "went up the mountain" and appointed twelve to extend his own mission of preaching the kingdom of God and healing and exorcism, it is unavoidably clear that Jesus is engaged in a renewal of Israel symbolized by the twelve as representative figures (3:13-19). The woman who had been hemorrhaging for "twelve" years and the young woman "twelve" years old whom Jesus heals are also figures representative of Israel undergoing renewal (5:21-43).

The sequence of episodes that follows the parables speech expands on the ways in which Jesus, as the new Moses and Elijah, is leading a renewal of Israel. Indeed this narrative step includes two sequences, each consisting of a sea-crossing, an exorcism, two healings, and a wilderness feeding (4:35–8:26). The sea-crossings suggest again a new exodus, and the wilderness is particularly suggestive of God's feeding of the people as they move along on "the way of the Lord," the twelve baskets of leftovers another symbol of Israel in its twelve tribes. The multiplication of food is reminiscent of Elijah's and Elisha's acts in their leadership of the renewal of the people in time of dearth. Jesus' healings, moreover, are reminiscent of Elijah, the great prophet of renewal. As if there were any doubt about Jesus as the new Moses and new Elijah, Mark then has the founding prophet of Israel and the renewing prophet of Israel appear with Jesus on the mountain to the inner circle of disciples (9:2-8).

Although it is often missed by readers, Mark also portrays Jesus as engaged in a renewal of the Mosaic covenant, picking up, as it were, where John left off in the story. The most explicit indications that he is engaged in renewal of the covenant come at two key steps in the story, the first as Jesus has completed his mission in Galilee and heads through Judea and up to confront the rulers in Jerusalem, and the other in his words over the cup in the Passover meal just before he is arrested (10:2-45; 14:22-25). In a series of dialogues, the first referring to the commandment prohibiting adultery and an ensuing dialogue quoting most of the covenantal commandments, Jesus gives what is in effect a "charter" of renewed covenantal teaching to his followers. His words over the cup at the Passover meal celebrating the exodus liberation, "this is my blood of the covenant, which is poured out for many," clearly referring to the basins of blood at the original covenant ceremony on Sinai, make the meal, which he will again celebrate in the kingdom, into a covenant-renewal ceremony (the term "new covenant" is in 1 Cor. 11:23-26, but not Mark 14:22-25).

Jesus' renewal of the Mosaic covenant that guided the life of Israel, moreover, is evident in several earlier episodes of the story. In his healing of the paralytic he faces head-on the misunderstanding of the covenant in self-blame for sickness, as he declares "your sins are forgiven" (2:1-10). As in John's baptism of repentance, Jesus' voiding of the punishment for sins gives the people a "new lease on life," empowering them to renewal of personal and community life. Significantly in the last episode before the parables speech, Jesus declares that the criterion of membership in the renewed familial community of mothers and brothers and sisters is "doing the will of God," which is a synonym in Israelite tradition for covenant keeping as well as for living directly under the rule/kingdom of God (3:31-35).

Throughout the story, but more dramatically in the climactic events in Jerusalem, Mark portrays Jesus carrying out his renewal of Israel in opposition to and by the Jerusalem rulers (and indirectly also the Romans). His healing of leprosy and forgiveness of sins provide an alternative to the Temple and priesthood. He speaks and acts with authority (power) in the interests of the people, in contrast with the scribes (1:21-28). In response to criticism by the scribes and Pharisees, he condemns their predatory practices of encouraging poor peasants to devote *(korban)* some of their produce to the support of the Temple establishment — thereby preventing the people from keeping the basic covenantal commandment of God (7:1-13).

Beginning with the entry into Jerusalem for the Passover festival, Mark portrays Jesus in one dramatic confrontation after another with the High Priests and elders and their representatives in the Temple courtyard (Mark 11–12). Jesus' journey to Jerusalem for the celebration of Passover suggests that his provocative actions and prophetic statements are a continuation of the new exodus in his renewal of the people. The people's cry of Hosanna (Save!) was part of the Hallel psalms (Ps. 113–118) that the people recited at Passover, which began by recounting the exodus and entry into their land. Mark mentions repeatedly that Jesus' actions and pronouncements against the rulers, supported by the crowds, were a threat to their rule (11:18; 12:12).

Because Jesus is usually thought of in Christian faith and theology as the Messiah and because he appears to enter Jerusalem in the posture of a popularly acclaimed king and is later crucified as "the king of the Judeans," it is often missed that Jesus acts and speaks as a prophet and even in prophetic forms in his confrontations with the Jerusalem rulers.

As indicated in his reference to Jeremiah's prophetic condemnation of the Temple (Jer. 7:11), his obstruction of business in the Temple is a symbolic prophetic act of (God's) condemnation. The clear reference to Jeremiah's prophecy against the Temple also indicates that the criteria for the condemnation are the same, the violation of the Mosaic covenantal commandments against oppression of the people. Jesus' series of confrontations with the rulers and their representatives are framed again by the prophetic declaration of the Temple's destruction (13:2). And in both the episode of the hearing before the High Priest and at the crucifixion, the accusation that he had threatened the destruction of the Temple is transparent to the poetic form of a prophetic oracle (similar to that in the *Gospel of Thomas* 71) in which the prophet announces the judgment (word) of God.

In the ensuing episodes as well, Jesus speaks in the role of a prophet. To the rulers' question "by what authority" Jesus is acting, Jesus replies with a counterquestion about the divine authority of John as a prophet (11:27-33), the implication being that he also had authority as a prophet from "heaven." The parable of the tenants of the vineyard (12:1-12) is not only a prophet's condemnation of the high priests in parable form, but the image of the vineyard of the Lord pointedly references the prophecy of Isaiah (5:1-7) about the vineyard of the Lord that condemned earlier rulers for their oppression of the people. The application of the analogy in the parable pronounces God's imminent action against the Jerusalem rulers as the tenants who have failed to care for God's vineyard, the people of Israel. The very question about the lawfulness of paying the tribute to Rome by the Pharisees and Herodians and their (false) flattery of Jesus (12:13-17) put him in the role of making a declaration about interpretation of the (first and second) Mosaic covenant commandments. He is the new Moses. And again the scribe's question and Jesus' reply about the "first" (greatest) commandment places him in this role of the giver of covenant commandments (12:28-34). Finally, both the form and substance of his warning to "beware of the scribes" is another prophetic statement (12:38-40).

Finally, again not often noted, Mark's story frames the high priests' arrest and condemnation and the Romans' crucifixion of Jesus with Jesus' continuation of his renewal of Israel. On the eve of his arrest and trial, he celebrates the Passover meal with a ceremonial renewal of Mosaic covenant, also giving instructions to the twelve to meet him back in Galilee. And at the empty tomb, the women are given the message to meet him in Galilee — evidently to continue the renewal of Israel that he had begun.

It seems clear from Mark's portrayal of Jesus that his overall program was the renewal of Israel against the rulers of Israel, and that Jesus' announcement of the kingdom and particular episodes of healing and exorcism, as well as controversies with the Pharisees and confrontations with the rulers, were particular components of that larger agenda.

The Series of Speeches in Q

By considerable consensus the earliest identifiable source for the mission of Jesus is the set of speeches of Jesus that are strikingly parallel in wording and sequence in Matthew and Luke. It has long been standard to refer to these as "Q," short for *Quelle* (the German term for "source"). Whether or not interpreters believe that the wording and sequence of Q as a document can be reconstructed, it is clear that Matthew and Luke have a good deal of Jesus' teaching, not derived from Mark, in parallel form and strikingly similar sequence.

Because of deeply ingrained habits in reading the Gospels, Q has been taken as a source of individual sayings, "the Synoptic Sayings Source." This classification persisted in the move by scholars eager to claim Q as an authoritative early "Gospel" source in the recent label "Sayings Gospel," by analogy with the much later *Gospel of Thomas* (as noted in Chapter 2). Most previous interpretation of these teachings of Jesus has thus fragmented them into individual sayings that thus lack indication of meaning-context. But, just as the canonical and other Gospels are now finally being recognized as sustained stories, the teachings of Jesus paralleled in Matthew and Luke are finally being recognized as a series of short speeches on matters of concern to a Jesus movement, at least by leading American scholars.[4]

---

4. John Kloppenborg, *The Formation of Q* (Philadelphia: Fortress, 1987), took the first step, seeing Q as a composed set of "clusters." Analyzed as speeches/discourses in

Not only does the teaching of Jesus parallel in Matthew and Luke take the form of speeches, however, but these speeches are poetic in form, with a sequence of parallel lines, and some of the speeches take traditional Israelite prophetic forms (such as woes and a lament). The field's standard focus on individual sayings and recent concern with establishing the early or original wording of those sayings have effectively blocked recognition of the poetic form of the Q speeches. By adapting recently developed sensitivities to the oral poetry behind what have been "transcribed" as prose stories in the fields of ethnopoetics and the ethnography of performance, we can hear and discern the sequence of parallel poetic lines that comprise most of the Q speeches, with their frequent repetition of sounds, verbal endings, words, and whole lines.[5] Indeed, features such as repetition of sounds and words and parallel lines that repeat the same idea in similar-sounding synonymous terms suggest that the Greek text of Q speeches is somewhat transparent to (an) underlying Aramaic version(s), bringing us closer to the Galilean ethos in which Jesus worked.

In view of the references to place-names (the villages/town of Capernaum, Chorazin, and Bethsaida) and to "those in fine raiment" living in "palaces" (evidently Herod Antipas), the setting of Jesus' speeches is Galilee, more specifically the villages over against Antipas' capital cities. Jesus' prophetic pronouncements against the scribes and Pharisees and against the Jerusalem ruling house do not require Jesus to be in Jerusalem. Galilee had been under Jerusalem rule for the hundred years prior to Jesus' birth, and was probably viewed among Galileans as the "capital" of the areas and people of Israelite heritage. The principal characters, besides Jesus himself and John the Baptist, are the people (of Galilee) whom Jesus addresses and

---

Richard Horsley, "Q and Jesus: Assumptions, Approaches, and Analyses," *Semeia* 55 (1991): 175-212. See now also Alan Kirk, *The Composition of the Sayings Source* (Leiden: Brill, 1998); James M. Robinson, "History of Q Research," in Robinson et al., eds., *The Critical Edition of Q* (Minneapolis: Fortress, 2000), pp. lxii-lxvi; and, for fuller statement, Richard Horsley with Jonathan Draper, *Whoever Hears You Hears Me: Prophecy, Performance, and Tradition in Q* (Harrisburg, PA: Trinity Press International, 1999), ch. 4, pp. 61-93.

5. Extensive analysis and presentation in Horsley with Draper, *Whoever Hears You Hears Me*, chs. 7-14.

the scribes and Pharisees and Jerusalem rulers. As in Mark, both God and Beelzebul/Satan figure in the accusation and response.

While it might be going too far to claim that Q has a "plot," the first several speeches do seem to follow an intelligible sequence of topics. The form of the speeches is usually prophetic in some way, thus presenting John the Baptist and Jesus in the role of a prophet like those of old, and the content of the speeches is mainly prophetic. First comes John the Baptist's prophetic declaration of the baptism of repentance, i.e., a renewal of the Mosaic covenant, and of the coming one who will baptize in Spirit and fire (Q/Luke 3:7-9, 16-17). Following the threefold testing of Jesus in the wilderness (Q/Luke 4:1-13), as Moses and Elijah had been tested in preparation for their missions, comes the longest speech, that of covenant renewal, recognizable from its adaptation of the components of the Mosaic covenant form, beginning with a declaration of new deliverance that offers the kingdom of God to the poor and hungry (Q/Luke 6:20-49). The covenantal blessings and curses had long ago been picked up by the prophets in their oracles of new deliverance and/or divine judgment. Then comes Jesus' response to the Baptist's disciples' question as to whether he is the coming one, that he is indeed the coming prophet expected to heal various forms of malaise and preach good news to the poor, thus fulfilling the longings of the people and linking the Baptist and himself in the coming of the kingdom (Q/Luke 7:18-28, 31-35). Like a new Elijah commissioning his protégé Elisha, Jesus then sends his envoys two by two to village communities to extend his own mission of preaching the kingdom and expelling demons (Q/Luke 9:57-62 + 10:1-15).

In the following speeches, the prayer he teaches his followers appeals for the fulfillment of the longings of the people and the promises of the prophets to bring the direct rule of God (versus rule of foreign empire) in which people would have sufficient food and live in mutual cancelation of debts, as in traditional Mosaic covenantal teaching (Q/Luke 11:2-4). In reply to the accusations (evidently of scribes and/or Pharisees) that he is working in cahoots with Beelzebul, he declares that his exorcisms are done "by the finger of God," clearly suggesting that a new exodus is thus underway in his exorcisms as manifestations of the direct rule of God (11:14-20). Then, in a traditional prophetic voice, Jesus declares woes against the scribes and Pharisees as God's condemnation for their role in facilitating the exploitation of the people and persecution of the new prophets (John and Jesus himself), just as their forefathers had killed the prophets of old (11:37-52).

The next speeches in the series focus on how to handle being dragged into court (12:2-9), and being single-minded in pursuing the kingdom of God despite desperate poverty (lack of food and shelter; 12:22-31). The prophetic forms are particularly striking in his declaration that the presumed "sons of the kingdom" (the rulers) will be left out in the banquet of the kingdom with the ancestors of Israel and the lament over the imminent destruction of the ruling house of Jerusalem (Q/Luke 13:28-29; 34-35). The prophetic parable about the great supper carries a similar indictment and announcement of punishment (Q/Luke 14:16-24). The declaration about the suddenness of judgment (Q/Luke 17:23-37) functions probably as a sanction on all the preceding speeches. In what appears to be the final short speech in the series, he charges his twelve disciples to establish justice for the twelve tribes of Israel under the direct rule of God. As is evident, most of the speeches feature "the kingdom of God" in a prominent position as the theme that unites the whole series.

In a form quite different from the sustained narrative of Mark, the series of speeches that were the source of much of Jesus' teaching parallel in Matthew and Luke portrays Jesus as a prophet engaged in the renewal of Israel in opposition to the Jerusalem rulers and their scribal representatives. As the speaker in these speeches, Jesus has the role of a prophet. What is more, in several of the speeches he represents himself (along with John) as the final prophet(s) in the long line of Israelite prophets, many of whom were killed by the rulers for their warnings. Baptizing with Spirit and fire is clearly an agenda of renewal of the people. He declares that his exorcisms are, in effect, a new exodus. He calls John's disciples to see the people's longings as articulated by earlier prophets being fulfilled in his actions and speech. Central in his program is the enactment of Mosaic covenant renewal in performative speech, as the new Moses. The petitions for sufficient food and (mutual) cancellation of debts in the prayer for the coming of the kingdom of God indicate just how concretely economic the renewal is understood to be. He commissions his disciples to extend his mission, as Elijah had commissioned Elisha. He also pronounces woes against the official representatives of the rulers, as Amos or Isaiah or Micah had pronounced God's judgment on the officers ("princes") of the kings. And he utters a prophetic lament over the imminent punishing destruction of the ruling house of Jerusalem, as Amos, Isaiah, and Jeremiah had done. But while the rulers stand under God's condemnation, the kingdom of God is happening as the renewal of the people of Israel in its ideal twelve tribes.

Thus in a sequence of speeches, material very different from the sequence of episodes narrated in Mark and with only a few overlaps of topics, Q presents a parallel portrayal of Jesus as a prophet pursuing the renewal of Israel in opposition to the rulers of Israel.

Assessing the Character of the Gospel Sources: Results of Recent Researches

That the whole Gospel of Mark (or John, etc.) and the whole series of Q speeches — and not mere text fragments — constitute the principal sources for investigation of the historical Jesus is confirmed by the remarkable convergence of results of several lines of parallel but independent research, such as text criticism, oral communication, and oral performance.

On the assumptions of print-culture in which biblical studies is rooted, investigators of the historical Jesus, like biblical scholars in general, have assumed that once the Gospels were written, they provided a stable form and wording of the teachings of Jesus in the sayings they looked upon as their (potential) data. Starting from the presumably stable form of a saying in Mark or parallel sayings in Matthew and Luke, they could work backward to an even earlier or perhaps original form of the sayings and, applying certain criteria, figure out which sayings were "authentic" (early/original/going back to Jesus). This whole apparatus of historical Jesus scholarship has been built up on the basis of the assumptions of print-culture. Jesus-scholars trusted (or simply assumed) that their colleagues who specialized in text criticism had sorted out a dependable (or at least "early") text of the Gospels from the variants in ancient manuscripts, from which reliable modern translations were made.

Recent research in text criticism and related but independent areas, however, has undermined and challenged the assumptions on which biblical studies in general and the elaborate apparatus of historical Jesus studies are based. It would require book-length studies to explore these researches and their implications adequately. But perhaps a brief review of the principal implications will enable us to discern the character of our Gospels as sources in ways that have not previously been evident.

In taking a closer look at early (often fragmentary) manuscripts of the Gospels, leading text critics have found that they simply cannot establish an early text of the Gospels from the extreme variation of the wording in the manuscripts. Not until the fourth century, after "Christianity" had become the established religion of the Roman Empire, did standardized manuscripts begin to appear. As leading text-critic David Parker says, "The further back we go, the greater seems to be the degree of variation."[6] The considerable differences among early manuscripts appear to be due, not to the way copyists copied already written copies, but rather to the adaptation of important teachings of Jesus to people's lives. Thus scriptural authority lay not in one version of the text but in multiple versions — in contrast to the previous print-cultural assumptions of text critics who took textual "variants" in early manuscripts as "tampering with the text" or "misquoting Jesus."[7]

But why or how was there such variation in the texts of the Gospels? Parallel but separate research may help explain this variability of the early manuscripts of the Gospels. As noted in Chapter 7, extensive recent research has confirmed earlier suspicions about just how limited literacy was in antiquity.[8] Oral communication was dominant throughout an-

6. David C. Parker, *The Living Text of the Gospels* (Cambridge: Cambridge University Press, 1997), p. 188.

7. Eldon Epp, "The Multivalence of the Term 'Original Text' in New Testament Text Criticism," *Harvard Theological Review* 92 (1999): 257-63; "The Oxyrhynchus New Testament Papyri: 'Not without honor except in their own hometown'?" *Journal of Biblical Literature* 123: 10; in contrast to Bart D. Ehrman, *The Orthodox Corruption of Scripture: The Effect of Early Christological Controversies on the Text of the New Testament* (New York: Oxford University Press, 1993); and *Misquoting Jesus: The Story Behind Who Changed the Bible and Why* (San Francisco: HarperSanFrancisco, 2005).

8. The standard works are William V. Harris, *Ancient Literacy* (Cambridge, MA: Harvard University Press, 1989), and Catherine Hezser, *Jewish Literacy in Roman Palestine* (Tübingen: Mohr Siebeck, 2001).

cient societies, even in scribal circles, and was the exclusive means of communication for ordinary people. Even in literate scribal circles, such as the Qumran community, moreover, texts were learned by oral recitation, becoming "written on the tablet of the heart," and then were recited from memory in a community.[9] The well-known passage in the Community Rule from the Qumran community near the Dead Sea gives instruction not for the *reading* but for the oral *recitation* of a book of Torah.[10] To correct the standard mistranslation:

> And the many shall watch in community for a third of every night of the year, to recite the writing [*lqrw' bspr*] and to search the justice-ruling [*ldwrs mspt*] and to offer communal blessings [*lbrk byhd*]. (1QS 6.6-8; my adaptation of the Vermes translation)

This same oral communications situation persisted throughout the diverse development of the Jesus movements and their consolidation into what became orthodox "Christianity." Just as authoritative books in Hebrew were recited in Judean scribal communities, but at a different social level, the Gospels, long after they were written down, were recited or performed in communities of Jesus movements. Traditions of Jesus' actions, practice, prophecy, and teaching were not simply transmitted from one person to another, but were used, applied, told, and retold in communities among which they resonated. This cultivation continued once the Gospels were composed and repeatedly performed in communities. And it is just this cultivation or use of the Gospels that explains the existence of multiple versions in diverse wording of the early manuscripts of the Gospels, as noted earlier.

This may be disturbing to those deeply embedded in the assumption of print-culture. But it is reassuring once we come to recognize that hearing or reading the whole Gospel story(ies) may offer a consistency or stability in our sources for Jesus that particular sayings turn out not to

9. David M. Carr, *Writing on the Tablet of the Heart: Origins of Scripture and Literature* (New York: Oxford University Press, 2005); Richard A. Horsley, *Scribes, Visionaries, and the Politics of Second Temple Judea* (Louisville: Westminster John Knox, 2007), chs. 5-6.

10. Martin S. Jaffee, *Torah in the Mouth: Writing and Oral Tradition in Palestinian Judaism 200 B.C.E.–400 C.E.* (Oxford: Oxford University Press, 2001).

provide. Studies of multiple oral performances of epic songs, ballads, poems, and authoritative stories in other cultures by scholars of oral performance in other fields are finding that while the words, lines, stanzas,
etc. vary from performance to performance, even with the same performer, the overall story generally remains consistent.[11] The overall text
has a certain integrity and consistency from performance to performance. If we extrapolate from these studies to the composition and early
repeated performances of the Gospels, it is clear that we should look for
stability or consistency in the principal sources for the historical Jesus in
the overall Gospel story or series of Q speeches, and not in particular
lines and verses (contrary to previous assumptions and procedures). Historical investigation into the historical Jesus in historical context requires that we take the Gospels whole as the sources, and not isolate on
text-fragments.

11. The best general discussion of research on cross-cultural studies of oral performance is John Miles Foley, *How to Read an Oral Poem* (Urbana: University of Illinois
Press, 2002).

CHAPTER NINE

Jesus Leading the Renewal of Israel
(Against the Rulers of Israel)

We should now be ready to use the whole Gospel stories and Q series of speeches as sources for investigation of the historical Jesus, following the relational and contextual approach outlined in Chapter 6. Recognition that our sources are sustained stories and a series of speeches and in repeated performance is germane to our historical inquiry. Recent studies of orally performed texts, and nascent theory of oral performance, have emphasized the importance, in understanding a text, of appreciating the performed text in its *context* as it resonates with the hearers by referencing the *cultural tradition* shared by performer and hearers.[1] This nascent approach to texts-in-performance corresponds to the first two aspects of the provisional approach sketched in Chapter 6 — consideration of both the historical context in which Jesus acted in interaction with others, and the cultural tradition out of which Jesus, in interaction with his followers, responded to the historical crisis they faced.

1. Although biblical studies has not prepared us to appreciate texts-in-performance, we may be able to learn from pioneering interpretation in other fields. Particularly helpful may be the work of John Miles Foley, drawing on performance theory and ethnopoetics, with special attention to the referencing of cultural tradition. Most helpful may be John Miles Foley, *Immanent Art: From Structure to Meaning in Traditional Oral Epic* (Bloomington: Indiana University Press, 1991); *The Singer of Tales in Performance* (Bloomington: Indiana University Press, 1995); and *How to Read an Oral Poem* (Urbana: University of Illinois Press, 2002).

Just in this connection with the context, however, it is necessary to do some further evaluation of the Gospel sources for the historical Jesus (in relationship in context). We have come to believe that the Gospel of Mark, the Q speeches, and the other Gospels were produced in and for communities of various Jesus movements that had developed in response to the mission of Jesus. If the "composition" of Mark's story and the Q speeches is dated about thirty to forty years after Jesus' mission, however, as Jesus movements spread into wider areas, Jesus traditions would have been adapted to new social contexts and a different cultural ethos. An obvious change was from the Aramaic of Jesus and his followers to the Greek of Mark and the Q speeches. That shift, however, does not entail a shift from "Jews" to "Gentiles," as in the standard (and unfortunately often essentialist) conceptualization. It has become increasingly clear in recent study of the Gospels that the Q speeches, the Gospel of Mark (like the Gospel of Matthew), and the Gospel of John all understand Jesus' mission and their own communities' identity as Israelite. The stories they tell and the speeches they give and the communities they address are part of the renewal of the people of Israel begun in Jesus' mission.

It is necessary to recognize the shifts and adaptations of Jesus traditions in the development of the Gospel texts. Yet two inappropriate extremes can be avoided in doing this. On the one hand, the diversity evident in Gospel and other texts undermines the credibility of the older scheme of a simplistic single-line development in stages from Jesus' teaching, to the "Easter faith" in the resurrection, to early Christian formulations later attributed to Jesus, to the writing of the Gospels as transformations or distortions of Jesus' original teaching in the light of the resurrection. New Testament texts cannot be fitted into a coherent developmental scheme. The view that Mark was written by a protégé of Peter for the church in Rome, for example, depends on Christian ecclesial tradition that accords with and supports later orthodoxy. Clues internal to the Gospel suggest rather that Mark's story was addressed to communities in Syrian towns and villages.[2] On the other hand, it is not credible sociologically to posit a separate community (and "Christology") for ev-

2. Explained in Richard Horsley, *Hearing the Whole Story: The Politics of Plot in Mark's Gospel* (Louisville: Westminster John Knox, 2001), chap. 2.

ery "source" supposedly used in the Gospels of Matthew and Luke or for every "type" of material identified in the Gospel, such as "the synoptic apocalypse" or "signs source."[3]

Shifts and changes in some Jesus traditions, however, can be discerned that will then help in discerning the continuity of Jesus traditions and context from the Galilean and Judean context of Jesus' mission to the respective contexts of Mark and the Q speeches. To make the presentation manageable we focus on only a few examples. Although Jesus' followers may well have experienced repression during the time of his mission, the fourth "beatitude" (and fourth woe, Q/Luke 6:22-23, 26) seems to be an adaptation to make this speech fit a later situation of a Jesus movement. Similarly, the statement drawing a distinction between speaking against "the Son of Man" and speaking against "the Holy Spirit" appears to shift the speech to address a situation after Jesus' own mission. Some (parts of) Q speeches (such as Q/Luke 13:28-29; 14:16-24) would have been easily susceptible of being construed as opposition to Israel generally and not just the rulers of Israel — as they (tragically) have been in Christian interpretation, even recently. Yet there is very little in the Q speeches that would not fit the context of Jesus' mission in Galilee. The Q speeches represent Jesus as a prophet who had died a martyr's death, like the prophet before him, yet know nothing about a resurrection and/or exaltation. And certainly the Q speeches know nothing of a mission to other peoples ("Gentiles") beyond Jesus' mission to the people of Israel.[4]

In Mark there are many more obvious adaptations to a historical context after Jesus' own mission. Jesus' speech in Mark 4 interprets his parables for a later situation. Jesus' speech in Mark 13 evidently ad-

---

3. A generation ago, prominent studies of the development toward the Gospels identified several sources that were then identified with particular communities of Jesus-followers/Christ-believers and thought to express particular christologies and their subsequent development. This is not only over-schematic but places more weight on fragmentary evidence than it will bear. See the collection of influential essays in James M. Robinson and Helmut Koester, *Trajectories through Early Christianity* (Philadelphia: Fortress, 1971).

4. The fragments in Luke (Q?) 7:1-10 are hardly sufficient basis for positing a "Gentile mission"; Matthew composes these fragments, along with Q/Lk 13:29, 28, into Jesus' prophecy of developments far beyond the mission of Jesus.

dresses the continuing historical situation in Judea in the decades following Jesus' mission. Mark's story clearly knows of Jesus' "resurrection" appearances, yet (not mentioning them) interprets them with reference to the disciples' meeting Jesus again in "Galilee" to continue his mission (14:28; 16:1-8). In two episodes Mark's narrative interprets Jesus' statements — about a "human one" having "authority on earth to forgive sins" and about the Sabbath being made for humanity — as referring to the authority of "the Son of Man," yet remarkably leaves Jesus' statements intact (2:1-12; 2:23-28).

Like the Q speeches, Mark also has Jesus traditions that are susceptible of later being construed against Israel (or "Judaism") generally, not just the rulers (as was done by generations of Christian interpreters). In Mark's narrative itself, however, the parable of the tenants is clearly told against the Jerusalem rulers, and the dispute over purity codes and *korban* was clearly against the scribal-Pharisaic representatives of the Jerusalem Temple. Like other misunderstandings of Markan episodes, these are the result of later Christian interpretation. The episode of the Syrophoenician woman does not imply a "Gentile mission," only that the renewal of Israel could include non-Israelites. Jesus' working across the frontiers of Galilee in the region/villages of Tyre and Caesarea Philippi may be the "footprints" of the later expansion of a Jesus movement, or may point to Jesus' own extension of the renewal of Israel across the frontiers of what were not necessarily ethnic divides but political jurisdictions imposed by Roman rule. In Israelite tradition, the people of Israel always had porous "boundaries," with peoples of various origins included in the covenantal society. In Mark 7:1-3, "the Judeans" is a geographical term. The story knows nothing of the modern Christian construction of "Judaism" in which there was a sharp separation between "the Jews" and the "Gentiles," as in some modern interpreters' projection of a "Jewish" side and a "Gentile" side of the Sea of Galilee. As with the Q speeches, so most of the episodes in Mark's story fit well in the context of Jesus' mission in Galilee and confrontation with the rulers in Jerusalem.

With such critical assessments of the sources we can, following the relational and contextual approach outlined in Chapter 6, investigate more closely parallel if different indicators in Mark's story and the Q speeches of key aspects of Jesus' interaction with followers and/or opponents. In this chapter we will focus on the indications of how, in the role of a prophet, he generated a movement of the renewal of Israel. In the next chapter we will focus on how his prophetic renewal of Israel was opposed to and by the rulers of Israel, resulting in his crucifixion by the Romans.

A Prophet Leading a Movement

Perhaps the best place to begin, in using our sources, is to consider the role in which they represent Jesus as acting. Abraham Lincoln acted in the office of President of the United States when the elite leaders of the southern states withdrew from the Union. The ancient Judean historian Josephus describes Simon bar Giora as acting in the role of a popularly acclaimed king in the midst of the widespread popular revolt against the Romans and their client high-priestly rulers in 67-70 CE. His accounts present Theudas as a prophet leading a movement of villagers to experience a new act of deliverance in mid-first century Judea. The different accounts of John the Baptist in Josephus and the Gospel of Mark both give indications that he was not just a prophet who uttered pronouncements against rulers (Herod Antipas in particular) but was leading a movement of renewal, a Mosaic covenant renewal focused on the baptism of repentance.[5]

In a somewhat analogous way, the very different representations of Jesus in Mark's story and the Q series of speeches both present him as a prophet leading a movement (of renewal of Israel). As noted (in Chapter 8), the Q series of speeches are delivered by Jesus in the role of a prophet, and several represent him as a prophet, explicitly or implicitly. This includes his killing by the rulers and their representatives, just as their ancestors had killed earlier Israelite prophets. Insofar as these speeches continued to be performed to communities of his followers, moreover, it

---

5. Laid out clearly by Robert L. Webb, *John the Baptizer and Prophet: A Socio-Historical Study* (JSNTSup 62; Sheffield: JSOT Press, 1991); Webb's analysis and presentation has led me to understand John more as a prophet leading a movement rather than a individual oracular prophet, as in Horsley with John Hanson, *Bandits, Prophets, and Messiahs* (Minneapolis: Winston, 1985).

is clear that Jesus must have been the catalyst of a movement. And in some of the speeches he speaks as leader of a movement, most noticeably in the covenant-renewal speech and the commissioning of envoys to expand his mission in village communities.[6] In contrast with the Gospel of Mark and particularly with the Gospels of Matthew and Luke, which represent Jesus also as a/the Messiah, while incorporating the series of speeches in their overall story, it is striking that the Q series of speeches give not even a hint of Jesus in the role of a messiah.

The Gospel of Mark also represents Jesus as a prophet of a movement, while struggling with or ambivalent about whether he was also acting as a messiah.[7] The Gospel of Mark has been read in traditional Christian theological terms as presenting Jesus as the Messiah, albeit as a suffering messiah who was crucified. But this reading still involved the synthetic Christian construct of "the Messiah" that incorporated the features of other figures or divine agents, such as "the suffering servant," "the Son of Man," and certain prophetic features. If we compare with leadership roles attested in contemporary sources such as Josephus, we find that the representation of Jesus in Mark's story is primarily as a prophet leading a movement. And in key episodes in the Gospel of Mark, Jesus himself rejects the disciples' misunderstanding of him as a popular king leading a revolt against the Roman imperial order. Most notably, after Peter pronounces that Jesus is "the Messiah" and then rebukes Jesus following his announcement that "the son of man" must suffer and die, Jesus in turn rebukes Peter: "Get behind me Satan" (8:27-33). Then in response to the request of James and John for positions of power in his kingdom, he makes the declaration about leaders as servants of the movement (10:35-45). It is not clear how he answers the High Priest's question, "Are you the Messiah, the Son of the Blessed One?" (14:53-65). The Roman governor Pilate crucifies him on the charge of being "the king of the Judeans," after which the Roman soldiers mock him as a king and the high priests mock him as "the king of Israel." In contrast with the charge on which he is crucified, however, the Gospel of Mark portrays Je-

6. This point is developed in connection with many of the Q speeches in Horsley and Jonathan Draper, *Whoever Hears You Hears Me: Prophecy, Performance, and Tradition* (Harrisburg: Trinity Press International, 1999).

7. Explored more fully in Horsley, *Hearing the Whole Story,* chap 10.

sus consistently through the narrative as carrying out his mission as a prophet leading a movement.

Because of the very different ways in which Mark and the Q speeches represent Jesus, it is thus all the more striking that both present him in the role of a prophet leading a movement. These portrayals of Jesus as a prophet leading a movement, moreover, fit very well in and have great credibility in the historical context. As laid out in Chapter 7 above, several prophets leading movements emerged in the immediate time-period in mid-first century Palestine, one among the Samaritans and several among the Judeans. And, judging from Josephus' accounts, all of these movements were *in-formed* by Israelite tradition, the deeply rooted memory of Moses and Joshua, the founding prophets of Israel in the events of the exodus and the coming into the land.

In the survey of the portrayals of Jesus in the earliest Gospel sources, Mark and Q, it was clear that Jesus was leading a renewal of the people(s) of Israel in opposition to and by the rulers of Israel. We can compare the respective portrayals of particular key aspects of Jesus as a prophet catalyzing a movement and assess how they fit in the historical context and the Israelite cultural tradition in which Jesus and his followers would have been rooted — and thus assess the general historical credibility of the sources' representation.

Healing and Exorcism: Manifestations of the Renewal of Israel

Perhaps the most prominent feature of Jesus' mission in Galilee and beyond in Mark's story is his performance of healings and exorcisms. Mark's story also portrays Jesus' healings and exorcisms as one of the principal reasons for the rulers' and their representatives' active opposition. The Q speeches simply assume that healings and exorcisms were prominent in Jesus' mission. Jesus points to his healings as manifestations of how he is "the coming one" announced by John the Baptist (Q/ Luke 7:18-35). And in his response to the accusation that he is in cahoots with Beelzebul Jesus asserts that he does exorcisms "by the finger of God," suggesting that they are manifestations of a new deliverance like that of the exodus (Q/Luke 11:14-20). That both Mark and the Q speeches include a version of the "Beelzebul controversy" indicates that this in particular was an early Jesus tradition and (thus, even if no such concrete "conversation" between scribal challengers and Jesus ever took place) that the power working through Jesus was (understood as) a threat to the rulers' control over the people.

Recent interpreters of Jesus, from Crossan, Funk, and the Jesus Seminar, to John Meier, rooted in the Roman Catholic tradition, insist that, because the tradition is so extensive in both sayings and stories that Jesus performed healings and exorcisms, he surely must have done them. Then after close analysis of every "miracle story" they find precious few "elements" that "go back to Jesus," leaving them skeptical about particular incidents. This standard focus on each story of healing and exorcism, however, constitutes a kind of atomizing positivist approach to history. In the relational and contextual approach we are attempting to develop here, we are asking different questions: How may the portrayals of Jesus' exorcisms and healings in whole texts (not text-fragments) point to what was happening in Jesus' interaction with people on the basis of Israelite tradition in their situation of crisis in Roman Palestine, and what may have been their significance in and for the movement he was leading?

As often noted in form-critical analysis, the episodes of healing and exorcism in Mark usually focus on only two characters, Jesus and the person seeking healing or the possessed person. These episodes, however, often involve others, relatives and/or friends who are concerned about and/or care for the person to be healed, as well as onlookers. Healing/exorcism happens in a social setting. In contrast to the individualistic orientation of modern interpreters, these episodes reflect the patterns of social relationships that would prevail in traditional agrarian societies such as ancient Galilee. Historically, illness and possession would have involved just such social networks — which in a crisis situation might well have been disintegrating under pressure of multiple layers of taxation, debt, hunger, self-blame (a sense of having sinned). Moreover, the healings often, explicitly or implicitly, involve *trust* ("faith," NRSV) in Jesus' power to heal by the relatives/friends and/or the person seeking healing, as exemplified especially in the hemorrhaging woman (5:21-43). In other episodes, such as that of "Jairus'" twelve-year-old daughter, it is the relatives or friends who trust that Jesus can heal.

Both of these aspects of the healing and exorcism episodes — along with the social relations and the people's trust in the healing powers operative through Jesus — illustrate how a movement would develop and why/how Jesus would have power to heal and exorcize. This is what is significant historically and this is what the historian needs to understand and explain. Jesus' role as a prophet in general and his healing and exorcism in particular were relational and contextual and were rooted in cultural tradition. Jesus could heal because the people with illnesses resulting from their circumstances were longing for healing and because they trusted that he could heal. The relational factors were multiple, and the explanation, which we can construct only in retrospect, may sound circular. As articulated in the first exorcism episode in Mark, Jesus' power (*exousia,* "authority/power") with the people developed partly from his healing and exorcizing people. But he could heal because he (already) had a reputation as a healer, which led people to trust in him. And, in another factor in this multidimensional relationship and explanation, the people's longings were informed by their memory of stories of Elijah's healing in similarly desperate circumstances of old. The healings and exorcisms happened as features of the broader movement, and the movement developed precisely as Jesus gained a reputation as a healer.

Such is the relational character of a historical movement. And the representations in Mark and the Q speeches have a certain "historical verisimilitude" with regard to the historical circumstances and the particulars of the Israelite tradition that informed Jesus and the people who responded to him in the role of a prophet. In Jesus' response to John's disciples' question (Q/Luke 7:18-35), his healings are a response to the longings of the people that the blind would see, the lame walk, the deaf hear, and the lepers be again integrated into the community, as had been articulated repeatedly in prophetic tradition (Isa. 35:5-6; 42:6-7; 61:1). The exorcisms are manifestations of the realization of a new exodus, the presence of the direct rule of God (Q/Luke 11:14-20). In Mark the healings and provision of food are reminiscences of Elijah's and Elisha's healings and provision of food. And Mark's story frames some of Jesus' healings and exorcisms (*dynameis,* "acts of power") with episodes of sea-crossing and feeding in the wilderness, clear reminiscences of the exodus and wilderness journey of Israel, signaling that Jesus' healings and exorcisms are part of a new exodus, a re-newal of the people.

Disciples, the Twelve, and the Mission of Envoys

Also key in the renewal of Israel in both Mark and the Q speeches are Jesus' recruitment of disciples, his appointment of the Twelve, and his commissioning of envoys to extend his mission of preaching and healing/exorcism to village communities. In Mark's story these are linked, indeed in narrative sequence (Mark 1:16-20; 3:13-18; 6:7-13). In the Q speeches, Jesus commissions envoys in one speech (Q/Luke 9:57-62 + 10:2-16), then addresses the Twelve in what was perhaps the concluding speech (Q/Luke 22:28-30). The Twelve are extensively attested early and in different strata of the wider Gospel tradition (including John) and Paul's letters and in various forms of material (speeches, narrative, creedal formula). But then later in the tradition references to the Twelve disappear, probably because they had no leadership position as the movement(s) spread and diversified. The sequence of narrative in Mark 1 (from Jesus' wilderness testing to calling disciples) and the sequence in the Q mission speech (from the images of the "plow" and not "looking back" to the sending of envoys) both allude to the prophet Elijah's commissioning of his protégé Elisha to continue his prophetic mission.

In both the Markan narrative and Q speeches the Twelve are symbolic representatives of the people of Israel that in cultural tradition had consisted of the twelve tribes. Both sources present the Twelve not as representatives of the particular twelve tribes, but as symbolic representatives of Israel (as a people generally) now undergoing renewal. In Mark this is clear from the other use of the symbol in the woman whose trust in Jesus results in her healing after hemorrhaging for twelve years, and in the almost-dead twelve-year-old girl whom Jesus brings back to life, both symbolic of the people of Israel. What was probably the concluding short speech in the Q series of speeches (Q/Luke 22:28-30) has been misunderstood and mistranslated according to the Christian theological scheme of the supersession of Judaism by Christianity, with the twelve "judging" Israel. The term *palingenesia* in the Matthean version (Matt. 19:28) has been misunderstood as "the renewal of all things" (à la Stoic philosophy), but means rather the restoration of Israel (in its representative twelve tribes, similar to Josephus' usage, *Ant.* 12.66, 107). Most important, the term *krinein,* understood in Israelite tradition in which God "defended" or "effected justice for" the poor, the orphan, and the widow, cannot mean "judge" (with its negative, condemnatory connotation). Rather in this speech Jesus is declaring that (in the kingdom) the Twelve will be sitting on twelve stools "liberating" or "effecting justice for" the "twelve tribes of Israel," the renewal of which they symbolize. This symbolism is deeply rooted in the wide Israelite tradition of twelve tribes/stones (of Joshua's covenant-renewal ceremony and Elijah's altar!)/pillars/bulls/ rams/lambs/goats/pieces of the prophet Ahijah's garment/etc., all of which represent the people of Israel.[8]

The commissioning of envoys to extend his own mission is one of only four subjects on which Mark and the Q speeches have closely parallel speeches (evident in how Luke follows Mark in Luke 9:1-5 and then Q in Luke 9:57-62 + 10:2-16). This indicates that the tradition of the commissioning was especially important to two parallel Jesus movements, and also early. Although it has been largely ignored, both of these versions of the commissioning are highly significant insofar as they fit the historical situation. Jesus sends his envoys to stay with families while working in village communities. In the agrarian society of Galilee, as we know from archeology as well as the historian Josephus, the fundamental social form was the village community, which consisted of a larger or smaller number of family households. And in this agrarian society with multiple layers of rulers, the families were subsistence farmers.[9] Again Jesus' instruction (in Q/Luke 10:7) to be content with eating whatever they have fits the historical situation of hunger and indebtedness (as in the Lord's Prayer as well). Just as the Twelve are representative of the renewal of Israel, so the commissioning of envoys is an implementation of Jesus' mission of the renewal of Israel.

8. Fuller discussion in Richard Horsley, *Jesus and the Spiral of Violence* (San Francisco: Harper and Row, 1987), 199-208.

9. Discussed more fully, with multiple references from various sources in Richard A. Horsley, *Galilee: History, Politics, People* (Valley Forge: Trinity Press International, 1995), esp. chaps 8-9.

While Jesus was evidently a prophet leading a movement similar to Theudas, the prophet (returned) from Egypt, the Samaritan prophet, and other prophets in the following decades, he thus differs from them in a significant respect. In contrast to these other prophets leading their followers out of their villages, Jesus evidently focused his mission on renewing the village communities that formed the fundamental social form of Israelite society. Jesus pointedly carried out his mission of healing and preaching in those village communities and their local assemblies (the meaning of the Greek term *synagōgai*).

Jesus' Renewal of the Mosaic Covenant

The Mosaic covenant stood at the center of Israelite tradition. It was, in effect, the constitution of Israelite society.[10] In its structure (as in Exod. 20; Josh. 24; Deut. 5; 27-28), it included God's deliverance of the people from bondage that was the basis of their commitment to God as their exclusive ruler, the fundamental principles of social-political life that guided social-economic interaction in the society, and ceremonial blessings and curses that motivated the people to keep the commandments. The covenant commandments were the criteria on the basis of which the Israelite prophets pronounced God's condemnation of kings and their officers for oppressing the people. Levitical and Deuteronomic law-codes adapted Mosaic covenantal laws and mechanisms such as sabbatical cancelation of debts and release of debt slaves as "regulations" to check abuse of power by rulers of the Jerusalem temple-state. The Qumran community by the Dead Sea understood itself not only as a new exodus community but as a renewed covenantal community, as stated in its guiding Community Rule (1QS). And of course it has long been recognized that John's "baptism of repentance (for the forgiveness of sins)" was a ceremonial renewal of the Mosaic covenant, in a ritual reminiscent of the exodus and a renewed commitment to God and the covenantal commandments.

10. More extensive discussion with extensive references in Richard Horsley, *Covenantal Economics: A Biblical Vision of Justice for All* (Louisville: Westminster John Knox, 2009), chaps 2-5.

Considering how prominent Jesus' covenantal teaching is in the Gospels, it is remarkable how seldom it is seriously discussed in books and articles on the historical Jesus. It is sometimes recognized that "the Sermon on the Mount" in Matthew 5–7 (or at least Matt. 5) is a covenantal speech. After all, Jesus delivers the speech on a "mountain," insists that "not one letter will pass from the law until all is accomplished," and then proceeds to "update" or rather "intensify" the commandments of the Mosaic covenant by declaring that "you have heard that it was said . . . , but I say to you . . ." (5:1, 18, 20-48). The parallel speech in Luke 6:20-49 has the same structure, and all of the sections of the speech in Luke also appear in Matthew 5–7. One suspects, however, that the focus on individual sayings prevents interpreters from noticing the overall structure of these speeches and/or imagining that Jesus taught in such patterns. Moreover, in the standard Christian theological scheme of Christian origins that determines much New Testament interpretation, Jesus and then Paul brought the gospel that replaced (or displaced) the (Mosaic covenantal) law of "Judaism." Both Mark's story and the Q speeches, our earliest sources, however, represent Jesus' renewal of the Mosaic covenant as the very center of his teaching.

Jesus' first and by far longest speech in the Q series, Q/Luke 6:20-49, is a covenant-renewal speech.[11] The core content of the speech, the section that begins with "Love your enemies," is full of the language and reminders of traditional Israelite covenantal teaching. Textual notes and commentaries contain numerous lists of the "allusions" or "references" to Mosaic covenantal laws or rulings in the Covenant Code (Exod. 21–23), the Holiness Code (esp. Lev. 18–19), and Deuteronomy. The speech, moreover, has the same basic structure as the principal texts of the Mosaic covenant in Exodus 20 and Joshua 24 (and Deut. 5; 27–28 — see the table on p. 124). As we shall see, the significant change is that Jesus transforms the blessings and curses into a new declaration of deliverance in the present-future. This transformation of the blessings and curses, which had previously functioned as sanctions on keeping the commandments, into a new declaration of deliverance in the present was also

---

11. More extensive analysis in Horsley with Draper, *Whoever Hears You Hears Me,* chap 9; and Horsley, *Covenant Economics,* chap 7.

Components of Covenant	Exod. 20; Josh. 24; Deut. 28	Q/Luke 6:20-49
declaration of God's deliverance	from bondage in Egypt	blessings of Kingdom
commandments to the people	ten commandments	love enemies, do good, lend
motivating sanctions	blessings and curses	parable: houses on rock/sand

done in the covenant-renewal ceremony outlined in the Community Rule of the Dead Sea community at Qumran (1QS 1–4). In both content and structure the covenant-renewal speech in Q/Luke 6:20-49 is thoroughly rooted in, indeed is an adaptation of, the continuing practice of Israelite tradition.

Often unnoticed is that the Gospel of Mark includes a somewhat similar renewal of Mosaic covenantal teaching in the series of dialogues in 10:2-45.[12] It comes at a significant point in the narrative, as Jesus completes his healing and teaching in Galilee and nearby areas and is heading into Judea and up to Jerusalem. It has previously been noticed that this series of dialogues include a series of law-like or commandment-like statements of principle in the form of "Whoever . . ." (10:11-12, 15, 43-44). Perhaps the clearest signal that these dialogues are renewal of covenantal teaching on key aspects of community life is the recitation of the Mosaic covenantal commandments in the first and third dialogues, on marriage and economic interaction, respectively (see esp. 10:19). Jesus' declaration earlier in the story that the familial community consists of "whoever does the will of God" (i.e., as in the commandments, 3:31-35) is also a restatement of the Mosaic covenant, as is his summary of the covenantal commandments in his later response to the scribe in the *two* greatest commandments (12:28-33). He also insists upon the primacy of the basic covenantal commandments of God, over against the Pharisees' "traditions of the elders" (7:1-13; to be discussed in Chapter 10).

On the basis of the prominence of renewed covenantal teaching in

---

12. Fuller exploration in Horsley, *Hearing the Whole Story,* chap 8.

both Mark and Q speeches, therefore, it appears that Jesus must have been engaged in renewal of the Mosaic covenant. Judging from the covenant-renewal speeches or dialogues in Q and Mark, moreover, this was a direct response to the crisis situation of the people in significant ways. Indeed Jesus' covenantal admonitions in the Q speech (Q/Luke 6:27-38) give indications of the dire situation of the people addressed. These admonitions address the desperate economic conditions in the village communities where hungry people had been borrowing and lending to one another (as admonished in traditional Mosaic covenantal teaching, e.g., Exod. 22:25-27; Deut. 15:7-8), and then coming into local social conflict when debtors were unable to pay back their neighbors who had meanwhile become desperate. This situation was the result of the multiple layers of rulers and their demands for revenues, tithes, and offerings for the priesthood and Temple, taxes for the Herodian kings, and tribute to Caesar. As indicated in the Lord's Prayer as well as in the beatitudes, the people were poor and hungry and heavily in debt. As they quarreled among themselves over debts and some families came under the control of creditors (see the "slices of life" in the parables of "the unmerciful servant," Matt. 18:23-35, and "the dishonest steward," Luke 16:1-9), the village communities that under less oppressive rulers would have provided a local "safety net" were beginning to disintegrate.

This disintegration of family and village community, the two fundamental social forms of society, also had a social-psychological aspect that went together with the social-economic aspect. Because the people were regularly reminded that if they kept the commandments they would be blessed in life but if they disobeyed the commandments they would be cursed, they tended to blame themselves for their poverty, hunger, and indebtedness. They and/or their parents must have sinned. This is the assumption on which John's baptism was based and one of the problems it addressed. The episode of Jesus healing the paralytic in Mark also attests this as a debilitating social-psychological self-blame among Galileans in the first century (2:1-12): the man is "paralyzed" because he had sinned (and Jesus' declaration that his sins are forgiven is tantamount to declaring that he is healed — he has "a new lease on life").[13]

---

13. See further the analysis in Horsley, *Jesus and the Spiral of Violence*, 181-84.

The covenant-renewal speeches, other covenantal teaching, and a covenantal ceremony are very prominent in both Mark and the Q speeches, deeply rooted in Israelite tradition, and parallel to other covenant renewal both at the scribal level (at Qumran) and at the popular level (John's baptism). And they directly address the crisis situation of Galilean villagers. It is thus virtually certain that covenant renewal was central in Jesus' mission. That this was happening in interaction with the people in those village communities is indicated in a seldom-noticed aspect of Jesus' covenantal speech. Both the covenant-renewal speech in Q/Luke 6:20-49 and the law-like statements at the center of the covenantal dialogues in Mark 10:2-45 are in what linguists call "performative speech." Pronouncing it makes it so, as when a judge in court pronounces "guilty as charged" or "not guilty" or when the Israelite prophets spoke "the word of the LORD" — and kings sought to silence them. "Jesus," through the performer of the covenant-renewal speech in Q/Luke 6:20-49, is enacting a covenant renewal in delivering the speech to a community of a Jesus movement. "Jesus," through the performer of the dialogues in Mark 10:1-45, is pronouncing (re-)new(ed) covenantal principles. Given the continuing re-performance of Jesus' teaching and prophetic pronouncements, we should not imagine that the Q speech or Markan speech gives us direct access to the actual words of Jesus. But it seems highly likely that the performative speech was a continuation of Jesus' practice in covenant renewal. In these speeches we are witnessing the continuing interaction of Jesus-speaker and Jesus-hearers that began in Jesus' mission in Galilean village communities.

In the covenant-renewal speech in Q/Luke 6:20-49, moreover, we can discern how this interaction of prophet and community may have "worked" in generating the renewal of the people/Israel, in at least two ways. As noted, Jesus transformed the blessings and curses into a new declaration of deliverance in the beatitudes and woes (blessings and curses) with which he begins the speech. Addressing people deeply despairing of their circumstances because they must have sinned, he declares, in performative speech that makes it so, "Blessed are you poor (hungry, mourning), for yours is the kingdom of God" (and "Woe to you rich . . .")! This not only parallels his declaration to the paralytic (Mark 2:1-12) in performative speech, "your sins are forgiven," giving people a "new lease on life." It offers them the direct rule of God, with its implications of deliverance from the oppressive Roman imperial order, by implication in the context of covenant renewal, reminiscent of the original deliverance of Israel from bondage under Egyptian rule.

Another important way that the interaction between the prophetic declaration of Jesus and disintegrating communities of hearers may have "worked" is evident in Jesus' renewed covenantal admonitions to "love your enemies, do good, and lend," in Q/Luke 6:27-36. To poor, hungry, mourning people who are "at each other's throats" in resentment over unrepaid loans, with insults and accusations, Jesus demands that they recommit themselves collectively to the covenantal principles and commandments of mutual cooperation and support in the village community. It is surely significant how this commitment to mutual cooperation and sharing parallels the Lord's Prayer (Q/Luke 11:2-4, but with the earthier, more concrete term "debts" in Matt. 6:12), in which the kingdom of God means concretely sufficient bread for subsistence and mutual cancelation of debts. It also parallels the speech in Q/Luke 12:22-31, where "seeking first the kingdom of God" would result in sufficient food and shelter, the context being the renewed covenantal community.

The series of dialogues that constitute a covenant renewal in Mark 10:2-45 also address the historical crisis of social-economic disintegration in Galilean-Judean society under the economic and other pressures of Roman rule. In sequence the dialogues address the disintegration of marriage and the family, membership in the community, economic exploitation versus mutual cooperation, and leadership in the renewal movement, all matters that the Mosaic covenant and traditional Israelite covenantal laws and mechanisms were concerned with. On marriage, Jesus insists on the rigor of covenantal commandments and laws versus the permissiveness of the Pharisees, whose laxity on divorce allowed Herod Antipas and other powerful figures to consolidate their political-economic power precisely through divorce and remarriage. Particularly striking is Jesus' insistence on the Mosaic covenantal commandments with regard to economic interaction (Mark 10:17-31). He pointedly uses the negative example of the man seeking eternal life, who was clearly wealthy, since ordinary villagers would have been concerned about where the next meal was coming from. He recites the commandments with the none-too-subtle substitution of "you shall not defraud" for ". . . not covet" to expose the man's exploitation of others economically, since the only way one could become wealthy in that (agrarian) society was by getting people in debt and charging high rates of interest. This is just what the high-priestly figures and Herodian rulers were doing under Roman imperial rule. The renewed covenantal principle, and covenantal sanction, comes in the declaration that it will be impossible for someone who is wealthy (from economic exploitation of the people) "to enter the kingdom of God." This is parallel to and equivalent of "Woe to the rich" in the Q covenantal speech. Significant is the concluding vision of the restored society that would result from economic cooperation as opposed to exploitation: restored families and their fields, albeit with persecutions. The ensuing "eternal life in the age to come" is a throw-away line, a closure-reminder of the opening of the dialogue: eternal life is a concern only of the exploitative wealthy.

In sum, from the portrayals in Mark's story and the Q speeches, it is evident that Jesus was responding to the crisis of Galilean and Judean society under Roman rule by drawing creatively on core aspects of Israelite tradition. As we know from Josephus' accounts of prophets leading movements and other sources, memories of Moses and Joshua as founding prophets of Israel, and of Elijah as the great prophet of renewal, were operative among the people in a way that informed the generation of extensive movements of resistance and renewal. In his interaction with Galilean villagers, Jesus adapted these formative social memories. His interaction with people in his healings and exorcisms in particular, reminiscent of those of Elijah and his protégé Elisha and generative of people's trust in the powers operative through him, would have been instrumental in the growth of a following that formed a widening movement. In contrast to other prophets leading renewal movements, however, rather than draw people out of their villages to experience a fantastic new act of divine deliverance, Jesus focused on the renewal of the village communities and their constituent families that constituted the fundamental forms of Israelite society. He commissioned envoys to further extend his mission of preaching and healing to village communities. And he proclaimed and performatively "enacted" renewal of the Mosaic covenant that had traditionally provided the basis and principles of local community interaction, mutual aid, and cooperation. This would also have strengthened the ability of village communities to resist the further encroachments and debilitating effects of the oppressive Roman imperial order in Galilee and Judea.

CHAPTER TEN

(Jesus Leading the Renewal of Israel)
Against the Rulers of Israel

———— ∞∞∞ ————

B oth the Gospel of Mark and the Q speeches present Jesus generating a renewal of Israel that is in opposition to the rulers and their representatives. In both early sources the Jerusalem rulers and their scribal and Pharisaic representatives seek to destroy Jesus, and Jesus pronounces God's judgment against them for injustice to the people. In this chapter, with our relational-contextual approach, we analyze and assess the earliest Gospel sources, with some attention to parallel traditions in other Gospels, to gain a clearer sense of how Jesus in the traditional role of a prophet interacted with the rulers, leading to his crucifixion by the Romans.

Jesus' Pronouncements Against the Scribes and Pharisees

The conflict between Jesus and the scribes and Pharisees was seriously misunderstood and misrepresented in standard New Testament interpretation for generations. On the basis of projections backwards from much later rabbinic literature, Christian scholars understood the Pharisees as representatives of normative "Judaism." They were supposedly the fastidious advocates of law-keeping, with emphasis on the casuistry of ritual law and purity codes. The Pharisaic defenders of the Law thus formed a foil for a Jesus who, in bringing the gospel, even purposely broke the Jewish law and criticized the Pharisees for their obsession with legalism. Serious attempts were made to correct this stereotypical theological scheme. But such magisterial surveys and interpretation of Judean and rabbinic texts remained within the frame of theological discussion or understood the conflict to be one of the differences between the nascent religion started by Jesus and the already functioning religious system of Judaism.[1] Recent Christian interpreters of Jesus have largely avoided dealing with Jesus' conflict with the Pharisees that is so prominent in the Gospels, partly because they have become acutely aware that they lack an adequate understanding of the sources (particularly rabbinic materials that may not after all provide direct evidence for the Pharisees, contrary to previous assumptions).

Another factor leading to this neglect has been the shifting understanding of the Pharisees (and scribes). In reaction to the Christian misrepresentation, the prominent scholar of rabbinic literature Jacob Neusner offered a highly influential portrayal of the Pharisees as having abandoned participation in the politics of the Jerusalem temple-state well before the time of Jesus and become a pious eating club focused on purity for their own table-fellowship.[2] Taking our cue more from a rereading of Josephus' accounts and extending the analysis to the political-religious function of the Pharisees in second-temple society, however, some of us suggested that the Pharisees had not withdrawn from the politics of the temple-state after all.[3] Rather, like other scribes,

---

1. See especially, from the Christian side of the discussion, E. P. Sanders's magisterial *Paul and Palestinian Judaism* (Philadelphia: Fortress, 1977); and *Jewish Law from Jesus to the Mishnah: Five Studies* (Philadelphia: Fortress, 1990). From the Jewish side see the many erudite books of Jacob Neusner, particularly *The Rabbinic Traditions about the Pharisees before 70*, 3 vols. (Leiden: Brill, 1971); and *Judaism: The Evidence of the Mishnah* (Chicago: Chicago University Press, 1981). Neusner criticizes Sanders for applying Christian theological categories to rabbinic materials. But Neusner himself finds in the Mishnah something like a philosophical-theological system of thought. And both take the texts as focused (narrowly) on religion.

2. Jacob Neusner, *From Politics to Piety: The Emergence of Pharisaic Judaism* (Englewood Cliffs, NJ: Prentice Hall, 1973).

3. Richard Horsley, *Jesus and the Spiral of Violence* (San Francisco: Harper & Row, 1987), pp. 15-18; Anthony Saldarini, *Pharisees, Scribes, and Sadducees* (Wilmington, DE:

they continued to serve as advisers to the high-priestly officers of the Temple, both under Herod the Great and under the Roman governors. In fact, as Josephus indicates, some of "the leading Pharisees" played prominent roles in the provisional high-priestly regime that controlled affairs in Judea and Galilee as well as in Jerusalem during the great revolt that erupted in 66 CE. As the professional guardians and interpreters of the official Judean tradition, particularly "the laws of the Judeans" that guided the operations of the temple-state, they were sometimes torn between their loyalty to the tradition and loyalty to the priestly aristocracy who were client rulers for the Romans. As discussed in Chapter 7, some circles of scribes sharply criticized and even mounted active resistance to the incumbent high priests as well as to Roman rule. Most, however, evidently continued in service of and representation of the temple-state.

Both the Q series of speeches and the Gospel of Mark portray Jesus as sharply condemning the scribes and Pharisees. The speech in Q/Luke 11:39-52 is a series of six woes and a declaration of God's judgment against them. Matthew expands these into a more elaborate condemnation of the scribes and Pharisees along with the whole ruling house of Jerusalem (Matt. 23). In the Gospel of Mark the conflict between Jesus and the scribes and Pharisees, who "come down from Jerusalem" to object to his statements and actions and to conspire with the Herodians how to destroy him, is an important subplot directly ancillary to the dominant conflict between Jesus and the Jerusalem and Roman rulers. But Jesus fires right back at their objections, and levels serious charges against them, two of which are particularly serious. One is that in keeping their "traditions of the elders," particularly in pressing the people to "devote" *(korban)* their needed resources to the support of the Temple, they reject the basic commandment of God (Mark 7:1-13). The other is that in otherwise urging the people to support the Temple with their meager "living" they "devour widows' houses" (12:38–13:2, note the narrative sequence).

The woes against the scribes and Pharisees have usually been inter-

---

Michael Glazier, 1988); and Steve Mason, *Flavius Josephus on the Pharisees* (Leiden: Brill, 1991); Horsley, *Hearing the Whole Story: The Politics of Plot in Mark's Gospel* (Louisville: Westminster John Knox, 2001), pp. 151-56.

preted as a debate about the Law/Torah or more particularly about purity laws. Recent interpretations find here a redefinition of purity in ethical terms (by taking Luke 11:39-41 and 44 as the key) or a radicalization of the Law (by taking 11:42 as the key). But only one of the woes even alludes to the Torah/Law (in the tithes of 11:42) and only two mention purity (11:39-41, 44, and then as a rhetorical device). Rhetorically, some of the woes mock the Pharisees for their focus on purity or their requiring tithes on every lit-tle herb. But the woes focus on the effect of the activities or role of the scribes and Pharisees on the people. They not only expect deference and seats of honor (11:43), but they "neglect justice" (11:42), "load the people with burdens too heavy to bear" (11:46), and in their practice of "extortion" have become a "danger" to the people (11:44), effectively preventing them from knowing how to keep the covenant (11:52; "entering the kingdom," Matt. 23:13). In "building the tombs/monuments to the prophets" they share the guilt of their ancestors who killed the prophets. God thus holds them accountable for the blood of all the martyred prophets (11:49-51, the sentence). The woes against the scribes and Pharisees condemn them for the debilitating effect of their political role on the people, particularly in regard to their advocacy of rigorous tithing, on top of taxes and tribute, and failing to use their scribal office to relax the burden on the people.

The key to understanding this series of woes may be to recognize their prophetic form and to appreciate the prophetic tradition in which they stand. As collected in the books named after them, the prophets Amos, Micah, Isaiah, and Habakkuk pronounced woes consisting of an indictment for violation of a covenantal principle and a statement of sentence or punishment. These they pronounced against the rulers or their officers for having exploited and oppressed the people. Some are single woes with statements of punishment. But many of the woes come in sets of two, three, or four, followed by a statement of sentence. Scribes critical of the priestly heads of the Jerusalem temple-state con-tinued the prophetic tradition of woes. Much closer to the time of Jesus, the dissident circle of scribes who produced the "Epistle of Enoch" (*1 Enoch* 94–104) pronounced several sets of woes against the high-priestly rulers and their scribes, with sequences of four or five woes (in-dictments for oppression of the people) concluding with a pronounce-ment of sentence.

Jesus' woes against the scribes and Pharisees in Q/Luke 11:39-52 thus stand in a long tradition of prophetic woes against the rulers and their officers. In substance they are reminiscent of Jeremiah's charge that "the false pen of the scribes has made [God's law] into a lie" (Jer. 8:8), and they continue the same basic form used by Amos, Micah, and Isaiah. As with other prophetic forms, moreover, the woes are performative speech, in which the pronouncement makes it so — regardless of whether the ostensible addressees are standing right there. The woes pronounced by Jesus thus functioned in the same way as those of the earlier prophets. They pronounced indictments for oppression of the people in violation of covenantal commandments and teaching, and they pronounced divine punishment.[4]

Jesus' most serious charges against the scribes and Pharisees in the Gospel of Mark are strikingly similar. On the assumption standard in New Testament studies (and more widely in modern western culture generally) that Jesus' "ministry" and the Pharisees were narrowly concerned mainly with religion, interpreters focus on the conflict over Sabbath observance and purity codes in Markan episodes. From early in Mark's story, however, these episodes focus on the role of the scribes and Pharisees as the enforcers of official Jerusalem's sacred political control of the religious-political-economic order. The scribes "come down from Jerusalem" to condemn Jesus for declaring that humans have the authority themselves to forgive sins — making the temple-apparatus unnecessary. And after a few more episodes, the Pharisees are conspiring with the Herodians (the corresponding officials in Galilee) to destroy Jesus (his healing and exorcism are clearly a threat to the official order). The religious-political-economic (structural) conflict between Jesus and his movement, on the one hand, and the rulers and their representatives, on the other, becomes most dramatic in Mark 7:1-13 and 12:38–13:2.

The conflict in Mark 12:38–13:2 is the more easily discernible in the charges and the narrative sequence. The ordinary people's resentment about the scribes' expectation of deference and honor that Jesus articu-

4. Fuller discussion in Horsley with Jonathan Draper, *Whoever Hears You Hears Me: Prophets, Performance, and Tradition in Q* (Harrisburg, PA: Trinity Press International, 1999), pp. 285-91.

lates, parallel to that in the woes (Q/Luke 11:43), was real, but it also had a concrete economic basis. The scribes were "devouring widows' houses," that is, their households, their family inheritance of house-and-fields. As illustrated in the widow who put two meager coppers into the Temple treasury, the scribes did this "devouring" by encouraging the people to donate their meager resources to support the Temple. This widow had just given away the mites that remained of her (and her family's) living, leaving her utterly destitute. In Israelite/Judean tradition, the widow and the orphan, as the poorest of the poor, were symbols of destitute people who were to be supported, according to the Mosaic covenantal principles and mechanisms, not further exploited. In narrative sequence this exploitation of the poor will result in (God's) destruction of the Temple of which the scribes are the representatives.

The parallel episode in Mark 7:1-13 begins, like some of the woes (Q/Luke 11:39-41, 44), with a mocking of the scribes' and Pharisees' concern about purity rules for eating. Far from representing Jesus as breaking "the Jewish Law," however, this episode has him insisting upon observance of the basic covenantal commandments of God. Moving to the more general level of the Pharisees' insistence upon the observance of their "traditions of the elders," the debate focuses on their role in late second-temple Judea of promulgating regulations that the people are supposed to observe that are not part of and go beyond "the laws of Moses" written on scrolls (Josephus, *Ant.* 13.296-97). This sets up Jesus' change of the subject from purity rules to the economics of fundamental subsistence for peasant families. By adhering to and advocating observance of their "traditions of the elders" the Pharisees are rejecting the basic commandment of God. How so? In urging the people to "devote" *(korban)* some of their land or its produce to the Temple, the Pharisees are preventing the people from keeping the commandment to "honor their father and mother," that is, support them when they are no longer able to be productive. The Pharisees were effectively draining away to the Temple the meager economic resources that remained to the people from which they could eke out a subsistence living.[5]

We should not imagine that this Markan episode reflects a particu-

---

5. Fuller exploration of this episode in Horsley, *Hearing the Whole Story*, pp. 166-72.

lar incident in "the life of Jesus." In fact, the narrative is shaped to explain to people beyond the ostensible setting in Galilee the practice of *korban* and how it manipulated people into rendering up desperately needed resources to support the Jerusalem Temple, something that Galileans would have been familiar with. Also, Mark's story is the only source for the scribes and Pharisees, who were based in Jerusalem, that represents them as active in Galilee — other than Josephus' accounts of Pharisees traveling to Galilee as representatives of the provisional high-priestly government during the great revolt in 66-67 CE. So it is unwarranted to suppose that the Pharisees kept Jesus under regular surveillance as portrayed in Mark 1–10 (or that Jesus dined with the Pharisees, as represented in Luke). Jesus' charges in Mark 7:9-13 and 12:38–13:2, however, so different in form from the woes in Q/Luke 11:39-52 yet strikingly parallel in the charges they bring, do indicate that Jesus, in his mission of renewal of the people, condemned the scribes and Pharisees for their role in draining away economic resources needed by the people to support the Temple.

Jesus' condemnation of the scribes and Pharisees, attested in both Mark and the Q speeches, fits the historical context in several ways. Scribes were "caught in the middle" between their loyalty to Israelite/Judean tradition of which they were the professional guardians, and the collaboration with their high-priestly patrons in Roman rule of Judea, although small numbers of them mounted organized resistance at certain key points (as recounted in Chapter 7). For the most part, however, Pharisees and other scribes played their mediating role in the Roman imperial order, provoking a level of popular resentment that we see clearly reflected in the mocking rhetoric of Jesus' charges against them. This popular resentment was displayed even against one of the scribal circles that offered active opposition to the high-priestly collaborators in Roman rule. As revolt erupted in the summer of 66 CE in Jerusalem, the Sicarii who had been assassinating high-priestly collaborators attempted to put themselves in the leadership of the popular revolt. The people, however, attacked them and drove them out of the city — whereupon the scribal group withdrew from the revolt and sat out the rest of the conflict atop the Herodian fortress of Masada. Jesus and his followers and (a generation later) the populace of Jerusalem were alike in their suspicion and condemnation of the professional representatives of the temple-state.

Particularly striking in its fit with the historical context is the reference to building the tombs of the prophets linked with the killing of the prophets in the series of woes and sentence in Q/Luke 11:47-51. Over two centuries before the killing of Jesus of Nazareth, the learned scribe Jesus ben Sira memorialized the prophets along with the kings and prominent priests of Israel/Judea as the great heroes of history in a paean of praise to legitimate the Oniad high priesthood, for which he was evidently a prominent ideological advocate (Sir. 44–50). As known from Josephus' accounts as well as archeological excavations, Herod the Great constructed or expanded a monument to the patriarchs and king David. He and other wealthy figures of the time were evidently also building monuments to the prophets.[6] The *Lives of the Prophets,* which stems from the first century CE, mentions monumental tombs and other memorials to many of the prophets.[7] The builders' motivation may have been a genuine piety, yet they also understood the political-cultural (propaganda) effects of such memorials, as they wrapped themselves in the aura, ironically, of the very figures who had pronounced God's condemnation on their predecessors in positions of power.

Nor was the irony lost on a contemporary prophet and his followers. As evident in the *Lives of the Prophets,* it was widely believed in the first century that many of those prophets of the past had been killed by the rulers they condemned. Herod the Great had been ruthless in eliminating anyone who criticized or demonstrated against his regime. And Jesus and his movement knew well what had happened to John the Baptist in response to his prophetic condemnation of Herod Antipas.

6. For a survey of Herod's building projects, see Duane W. Roller, *The Building Program of Herod the Great* (Berkeley: University of California Press, 1998); Peter Richardson, *Herod: King of the Jews and Friend of the Romans* (Columbia: University of South Carolina Press, 1996), ch. 8.

7. David Satran, *Biblical Prophets in Byzantine Palestine: Reassessing the Lives of the Prophets* (Leiden: Brill, 1995), argues that the *Lives of the Prophets* is a much later, mainly Christian document. Ana Maria Schwemer, *Studien zu den Frühjüdischen Prophetenlegenden Vitae Prophetarum,* 2 vols. (Tübingen: Mohr Siebeck, 1995), esp. 1:65-71, counters with compelling arguments for dating most of the material in the document prior to 70, while recognizing later Christian additions.

Jesus' Prophetic Pronouncements
Against the Temple and High Priests

Jesus' sustained confrontation with the high priests and their representatives forms the climax of Mark's story of Jesus' renewal of Israel
in opposition to and by the rulers of Israel, to which they respond by
surreptitiously arresting him and handing him over to the Roman governor for crucifixion. While Matthew and Luke follow Mark's narrative, the whole evidently independent narrative in the Gospel of John
focuses on Jesus' repeated challenge to "the Judeans" (not "the Jews"),
by which is meant mainly the high priests and Pharisees, at festival
times in the Jerusalem Temple. Mark's story is not taken seriously as a
reflection of an actual sequence of events at Passover time in Jerusalem. But Mark's narrative of the confrontation in Jerusalem and the
"passion narrative" in Mark include Jesus traditions indicative of Jesus'
pronouncements or actions against the Temple and high priests, some
of which have parallels in John and the *Gospel of Thomas*. Significantly,
moreover, one of the Q speeches includes a prophecy of Jesus against
the Jerusalem ruling house and a parable evidently directed against
the high priests.

To understand these traditions it is necessary first to bypass the
older Christian construct of a monolithic "Judaism" from which Jesus
and early "Christianity" supposedly departed, and rather to take note
of the more conflictual historical context and Israelite tradition. Long
before the Romans conquered Judea and Galilee, the Jerusalem temple-
state and its incumbent rulers who held their positions of power and
wealth in subordination to a succession of imperial regimes had been
opposed by both scribal circles and by popular revolt. The legitimacy of
the temple-state was further weakened by Herod's subordination of
Temple and high priesthood to his own regime, and the Romans' instal-
lation of high-priestly families that Herod had elevated to be their client rulers after his death. The high-priestly families' close collaboration with the Romans, against the interest of the people, and their
own predatory oppression of the people contributed heavily to the increasing social unrest, according to Josephus' accounts. This is the
worsening situation in which Jesus and other prophets emerged as

leaders of popular movements of renewal and resistance in the mid-first century CE.[8]

In addition to the memories of Moses and Joshua as founding prophets and of Elijah as the prophetic leader who challenged the oppressive rule of Ahab and Jezebel, Israelite tradition included oracular prophets such as Amos and Jeremiah. They prophesied not only against kings and their officers' exploitation in violation of Mosaic covenantal commandments, but condemned the royal temples, their lavish ceremonies, and the false sense of security they provided the wealthy and powerful (e.g., Amos 4:4-5; 5:21-24; Mic. 2:1-5; Isa. 3:13-15; Jer. 7:5-10). Best known, perhaps, was Jeremiah's pronouncement of God's unconditional condemnation of the Temple and priesthood for violation of the Mosaic covenantal commandments (parallel versions in Jer. 7 and 26). Contrary to a certain construction of "Jewish restoration theology," no expectation of a rebuilt temple is evident in Judean prophetic and apocalyptic texts.[9] In fact, implicitly or explicitly, apocalyptic texts do not include a temple ("tower") in their brief visions of a restored people ("house"). Haggai (first), Zechariah, and Malachi, of course, had been advocates for the building of the second Temple. Based on the prophecy of Elijah-Elisha, Amos, Micah, and Jeremiah, however, the role of the prophet was to condemn rulers and their officers for injustices in violation of the Mosaic covenant. And this is just what John the Baptist had done in oracles immediately before Jesus, and what the prophet (who had returned) from Egypt had done in collective action a few years after Jesus (in anticipating that the walls of Jerusalem would collapse, giving the people access to the city).

The presentations in Mark and the Q speeches of Jesus as a prophet include several traditions of his prophetic pronouncements against the

---

8. See further Richard Horsley, "High Priests and the Politics of Roman Palestine: A Contextual Analysis of the Evidence in Josephus," *Journal for the Study of Judaism* 17 (1986): 23-55; Martin Goodman, *The Ruling Class of Judea: The Origins of the Jewish Revolt Against Rome A.D. 66-70* (Cambridge: Cambridge University Press, 1987); Horsley, *Jesus and Empire* (Minneapolis: Fortress, 2003), chs. 1-2.

9. Versus E. P. Sanders, *Jesus and Judaism* (Philadelphia: Fortress, 1995), chs. 2-3; criticism in Horsley, *Jesus and the Spiral of Violence*, pp. 189-91. See now the critical analysis of key texts in *1 Enoch* in Horsley, *Scribes, Visionaries, and the Politics of Second Temple Judea* (Louisville: Westminster John Knox, 2007), ch. 8.

Temple, prophetic parables told against the high priests, and an account of a prophetic demonstration against the Temple and its rulers.

Jesus' prophecy against the ruling "house" of Jerusalem in Q/Luke 13:34-35a is almost verbatim in Matthew's and Luke's parallel texts, suggesting that neither changed it from the tradition they used.[10] The images in the oral poetry are almost palpable, with a mournful repetitive address, parallel lines with parallel sounds, and God as a protective mother hen.

> O Jerusalem, Jerusalem!
> You kill the prophets
> and stone those sent to you.
> How often would I have gathered your children together
> As a hen gathers her brood under her wings,
> And you refused.
> Behold your house is forsaken!
> For I tell you:
> You will not see me until you say:
> "Blessed is he who comes in the name of the Lord." (Q 13:34-35)

In this oracle, Jesus adapts the traditional form of a prophetic lament in which the prophet speaks the words of God. Amos 5:2-3, 16-17 offers a classic example, in which God's lament anticipates the future lamentation of the ruling city when judgment is finally executed. Similarly, in anticipation of God's imminent judgment, Jesus announces that Jerusalem is already desolate (because destroyed) and in mourning. Adding to the likelihood that Jesus of Nazareth continued this tradition of prophetic lament is the similar lament over the imminent destruction of Jerusalem thirty years later by another rustic prophet, Jesus son of Hananiah, as recounted by Josephus (*War* 6.300-309).

Jesus' portrayal of God protecting her children as a mother hen gathers her brood under her wing taps into a traditional image familiar from the "Song of Moses," a celebration of the exodus deliverance and covenantal formation of Israel. In this song God is "like an eagle that

10. Fuller discussion in Horsley, *Jesus and the Spiral of Violence*, pp. 300-304; *Jesus and Empire*, pp. 87-91.

stirs up its nest and hovers over its young, spreading its wings" (Deut. 32:11). In Jesus' lament, God as a mother hen is grieving because, even though she had tried to protect her children, the Jerusalem rulers had exploited them; hence their destruction was already underway.

Jesus' principal charge in this prophecy, that Jerusalem habitually kills the prophets God has sent, like the same charge in the woes, reverberates with Israelite tradition. Ahab and Jezebel attempted to assassinate Elijah (1 Kings 19; 18:17). King Jehoiakim even sent agents to Egypt to kill the prophet Uriah son of Shemiah. And after Jeremiah pronounced God's condemnation of the Temple, officials tried to lynch him (Jer. 26:7-23). Legends about the prophets in the later *Lives of the Prophets* suggest that Jesus' contemporaries believed that most of the prophets had been martyred for their message. And Herod Antipas had just recently beheaded John the Baptist for his insistence on covenantal justice (Josephus, *Ant.* 18.116-19; cf. Mark 6:17-29).[11] "House" was a standing term for a monarchy, dynasty, or temple-state with its whole governing apparatus, and also resonated with a long prophetic tradition of declarations of judgment against Jerusalem rulers, such as Jeremiah's pronouncement of judgment on the house of David (22:1-9). The severity of the indictment-and-condemnation that Jesus announces here should not be missed. God has already condemned Jerusalem as the ruling house of Israel.

The last line of the lament (Luke 13:35) recites a key line of the highly familiar Passover psalm (Ps. 118), giving thanks for previous deliverance and appealing for future salvation: "Hosanna! Deliver us!" God, speaking through Jesus, declares to the Jerusalem rulers that they will not see him until they welcome "the one who comes in the name of the LORD," presumably Jesus himself. But of course they were not about to do that. Since they have refused/forsaken God, they are about to be refused/forsaken by God.

Three different episodes in Mark cite or refer to Jesus' prophesying

---

11. In other cases, mentioned in Chapter 7 above, the Roman governors quickly sent out the military to slaughter such figures as the "Egyptian" prophet who returned to Judea to lead his followers up to the Mount of Olives. And just before the great revolt in 66 the high priests sought to have Jesus son of Hananiah executed, even though the Roman governor Albinus thought he was merely a maniac (Josephus, *Ant.* 20.169-71; *War* 2.261-63; 6.300-309).

against the Temple. Jesus' statement in Mark 13:1-2 that "not one stone will be left here upon another, all will be thrown down" is usually taken as a prophetic reference to the destruction of the Temple. Witnesses at his trial in Mark say they heard him say, "I will destroy this temple that is made with hands and in three days I will build another, not made with hands" (Mark 14:58). Passersby at his crucifixion deride him, saying "Aha! You who would destroy the temple and build it in three days . . ." (15:29). These reports have parallels in other Gospels. The simplest reference is in the *Gospel of Thomas* 71: "Jesus said: 'I shall de[stroy this] house, and no one will be able to build it [again],'" which is close to the "reports" in Acts 6:13-14 that Stephen had said "that this Jesus of Nazareth will destroy this place." That Jesus had prophesied destruction (and rebuilding) of the Temple was so deeply embedded in Jesus tradition that (to explain it away) the Gospel of John carefully had Jesus making reference to his body rather than suppress the prophecy (cf. John 2:19-21).[12]

Several modern attempts have been made to explain (away) this prophecy. Some have argued that at Jesus' trial in Mark the paraphrase of his prophecy is presented as false testimony. Mark's narrative ("But even on this point their testimony did not agree," 14:59) does not really say that. The assumption at the crucifixion scene is that Jesus had indeed spoken about destroying the Temple. And Mark's narrative had earlier represented Jesus as declaring that the stones would all "be thrown down." The witnesses' testimony is that Jesus himself would destroy the Temple. But if he had been uttering prophecy as the mouthpiece of God in the same way that earlier Israelite prophets had done, and in the same way as in Q/Luke 13:34-35, then it was God who was about to destroy the Temple.

The form of the prophecy in Mark 14:58 and 15:29 (and in John 2:19-21) is a double saying, about the destruction and the rebuilding of the Temple. The temple "not made with hands" was taken as a "spiritual" or "heavenly" temple in earlier Christian interpretation. The appearance of "house" in the *Gospel of Thomas* version, however, suggests another possibility for understanding the prophecy in its double-saying form. "House (of God)" was used in second-temple Judean texts not only for

---

12. Fuller exploration in Horsley, *Jesus and the Spiral of Violence*, pp. 292-300.

the Temple and for the ruling house but also for the people, and often for the restored people of Israel. Terms such as "house," "temple," "body," and "assembly" could all function as synonyms, usually with reference to a social body (the people). The community at Qumran near the Dead Sea, for example, understood itself as the (true) "temple" (1 QS 5:5-7; 8:4-10; 9:3-6; 4QFlor 1:1-13).

Jesus' prophecy of destroying and rebuilding the Temple can thus be understood as playing on the double meaning of the term "temple" or (more likely, as in the *Gospel of Thomas* version) "house." His prophecy declared that God was destroying the/God's "house/temple made with hands" in Jerusalem but rebuilding the/God's "house/temple not made with hands," the people of Israel. This was the agenda of Jesus' mission, as attested in Q as well as Mark, of spearheading a renewal of Israel in opposition to its rulers. If the renewed people itself were understood as the rebuilt "temple" or "house" of God, then of course there would be no need for a temple-state, which was widely resented among the people.

Mark's Gospel and the Q speeches each also include a parable that functions as a prophetic announcement of God's judgment against the high-priestly rulers. Again Jesus is operating in the tradition of Israelite prophets. The best-known prophetic use of a parable as a pronouncement of judgment against a ruler was Nathan's parable of "the poor man's lamb" told directly to David in condemnation of his abuse of royal power in the adultery with Bathsheba and the murder of her husband Uriah (2 Sam. 11–12). The parable of the great banquet in Q/Luke 14:16-24 was linked with, and perhaps part of the same speech with, Jesus' prophetic lament over Jerusalem's ruling house and evidently introduced by his prophecy of the people of Israel gathered from all directions for the great banquet of fulfillment in the kingdom of God with the ancestors and the prophets (Q/Luke 13:28-29). Framed by these prophecies, the wealthy, well-placed invitees in the parable who are too busy expanding their wealth to accept the invitation represent the powerful ruling families in Jerusalem, while the riffraff brought into the banquet at the last minute represent the ordinary people.

Simply in the context of Roman Judea, but especially as framed in the series of confrontations between Jesus and the high-priestly rulers in Mark 11–12, the parable of the tenants functions as a prophetic pronouncement of God's judgment against the high priests. Building on Isaiah's well-known prophecy about the people of Israel as God's vineyard (Isaiah 5), this allegorical parable presents the tenants of the vineyard (the high priests charged with care of the vineyard) as utterly irresponsible, manipulative, and violent to the owner and his messengers (God and the prophets). It would have been clear to the hearers, both to the high priests, who had built up large estates by forcing their debtors to become tenants, and to the ordinary people, whose neighbors had been forced into tenancy for their debts, what the master of the vineyard would do: get rid of the exploitative tenants, the high-priestly tenants of the Lord's vineyard, and give the vineyard of Israel and its land back to the people to whom it rightfully belonged.[13]

In prophesying against the Temple and high priests, of course, Jesus was also opposing the Roman imperial order, insofar as the Temple and high-priestly families were the very face of Roman rule in Judea. The Markan narrative sequence in Jesus' confrontation with the rulers of Israel fits the political logic implicit in Jesus' demonstration against the Temple and his parable pronouncing God's condemnation of the high-priestly "tenants." In opposing the Jerusalem rulers, Jesus is by implication opposing Roman rule. The obvious next step for the Pharisaic and Herodian representatives of the Roman client rulers of Judea and Galilee is to entrap him on whether it is lawful to pay tribute to Caesar. They can set the trap because they know full well that paying tribute to Caesar is directly against the first and second commandment of the Mosaic covenant. But the Romans took refusal to render up the tribute as tantamount to insurrection. If Jesus answers directly as well as truthfully, he can be seized for rebellion against Roman rule. In addition to exposing the Pharisees' and Herodians' violation of the commandments by having a coin with Caesar's image on it, however, Jesus formulates an answer that escapes the trap by indirection but indicates to everyone listening the very core of the commandments: "Give to Caesar the things that are

---

13. For further discussion of the separate (yet related) research on the interrelated issues in this section, see Richard A. Horsley, "Oral Communication, Oral Performance, and New Testament Interpretation," in *Method and Meaning: Essays on New Testament Interpretation in Honor of Harold W. Attridge,* ed. Andrew B. McGowan and Ken Harold Richards (RBS 67; Atlanta: Society of Biblical Literature, 2011), pp. 125-56.

Caesar's, and to God the things that are God's." In Israelite covenantal tradition all things belong to God, Israel's exclusive Lord, and Israel is not to "bow down and serve any other god/lord" with produce needed for the support of families. The scribal and Pharisaic leadership of the "fourth philosophy" had taken the same adamant stance over two decades before in organizing refusal to pay the tribute (as noted in Chapter 7).[14]

Why Was Jesus Crucified? A Prophet Leading a Movement and/or the Disruption of the Temple

The extent, the diversity, and the traditional prophetic forms of these prophecies and prophetic parables indicate that a major aspect of Jesus' mission consisted of pronouncement of God's judgment against the ruling institution and its high-priestly rulers in Jerusalem. These prophetic pronouncements, moreover, fit into the historical situation of escalating conflict between the high-priestly and Herodian rulers and the people during the first century. And they are paralleled by other prophets' pronouncements against or prophetic laments over ruling houses, that of John the Baptist just before and Jesus son of Hananiah a few decades after. John was arrested and beheaded by Antipas, ruler of Galilee and Perea. Judging from the minimal, mainly mocking criticism of Antipas ("that fox," "living in royal palaces in fine raiment," Luke 13:31-33; Q/Luke 7:25), Jesus of Nazareth had evidently steered clear of confrontation with Antipas, and focused his condemnation on the rulers in Jerusalem. The case of Jesus son of Hananiah, however, makes us doubt whether even the sharp condemnations of the Jerusalem rulers by Jesus of Nazareth would have led to his crucifixion by the Romans.

Jesus son of Hananiah also delivered prophetic laments pronouncing doom on Jerusalem, repeatedly and for years, in the hearing of the high-priestly aristocrats themselves. The latter, knowing well the resonance that such prophetic pronouncements had with the people, had him arrested and turned him over to the Roman governor, just as their predecessors evidently had in the case of Jesus of Nazareth. But the Ro-

---

14. Fuller exploration in Horsley, *Jesus and the Spiral of Violence*, pp. 306-17.

man governor apparently thought that such prophecies were merely mania, a nuisance but not a serious challenge to the Roman imperial order warranting execution by crucifixion. He merely had him beaten and released, whereupon Jesus son of Hananiah resumed his Jeremiah-like prophecy of doom against Jerusalem. In what way was Jesus of Nazareth, by contrast, so much of a challenge to the Jerusalem temple-state that the local representative of the Roman imperial order, Pontius Pilate, had him crucified?

If we work critically through our sources in the context of our increasingly precise knowledge of the historical situation, particularly of the high-priestly and Roman rulers, popular protests and movements, and the dynamics of Passover celebration in the Jerusalem Temple, the Roman order of crucifixion for Jesus could have one or both of two historical explanations: Jesus appeared to be a threat to the Roman imperial order in Judea insofar as he was generating a movement. And/or, he not only prophesied against the temple-state, but carried out a disruptive prophetic demonstration symbolizing God's condemnation of the temple-state.

Jesus son of Hananiah was, to judge from Josephus' account, a solitary oracular prophet, like Amos or Jeremiah before him, different from Elijah and Elisha, who worked with a wider circle of prophets, evidently in relation with the people even more widely (and eventually generating an uprising). In the accounts of Jeremiah's prophetic career, some of the ruling elite wanted to lynch him; others took severely repressive measures, and he was merely imprisoned or thrown into cisterns (Jer. 7; 26; 37–38). John the Baptist evidently generated a renewal movement among the people that was threatening to Antipas' control in Perea, across the Jordan, and/or Galilee — and was arrested and killed. Our Gospel sources, as analyzed above, indicate that Jesus of Nazareth also generated a movement of renewal and resistance among the people, although it was not as visibly disruptive as the movements led by Theudas or other popular prophets. In the Q speeches, Jesus' mission and movement appear to have been based mainly in eastern Galilee along the lake. It is difficult to judge from Mark's narrative of the extension of Jesus' mission into surrounding areas beyond the frontiers of Galilee whether this happened during Jesus' own mission or in its continuation after the crucifixion. Mark does represent Jesus as active in Judea on his way toward

Jerusalem. And although rarely noted, John's Gospel portrays Jesus as working actively among the people in every area of Israelite heritage, in Samaria and the trans-Jordan as well as in Galilee, but primarily in Judea. If John's portrayal is not merely projection back to the mission of Jesus, then perhaps Jesus worked for a time in Judea as well as Galilee. And even if Jesus' own mission had generated a movement primarily in Galilee, as suggested in Mark and the Q speeches, it may well have been known in Jerusalem, even though the temple-state no longer had direct political jurisdiction over Galilee during the lifetime of Jesus.

The other (or additional) historical explanation rooted in sources and circumstances would be that Jesus did not just prophesy against the temple-state, but mounted a disruptive prophetic demonstration in the Temple during the Passover Festival. The Q speeches know nothing of such a demonstration or that Jesus was killed specifically by crucifixion. Matthew and Luke follow Mark's narrative of the demonstration, while reducing its severity somewhat, and the direct connection between Jesus' disruptive action and the high priests' finally plotting to arrest him (Mark 11:15-19; 14:1-2 and parallels). John's narrative makes Jesus' demonstration in the Temple more disruptive and focuses the whole story of Jesus' mission on his repeated confrontation with "(the rulers of) the Judeans," i.e., the high priests and Pharisees at the festivals in the Jerusalem Temple. Whatever particular elements of historical verisimilitude might be found in them, it is unwarranted to place much credence in the details of Mark's episodes, such as the hearing before the high priests. Nevertheless on a more general level, it is clear from what we know of the Roman and high-priestly rule of Judea that a demonstration in and against the Temple would have been viewed as a challenge to the imperial order. This is true even if the demonstration were much more modest than portrayed in Mark and John and somewhat "disguised" in the crowded festivities of the celebration of Passover.

Nor would either the high priests or Pilate have been wrong in seeing in Jesus' temple-action a challenge to the Roman imperial order. From the way it is presented in Mark and in John, it is an obvious climax of Jesus' mission as a prophet generating a renewal of Israel, and it fits the historical context of conflict between the people and their rulers in the milieu of Israelite heritage.

As indicated in both Mark and the Q speeches, in his interaction with the people in healings and covenant renewal, Jesus had adapted the role of a prophet leading a movement of renewal. The role of such, as a new Moses or Elijah in Israelite tradition, like that of a new Jeremiah as well, included symbolic prophetic action or demonstration as well as pronouncements against oppressive rulers. Elijah had restored the service of Yahweh by a renewed Israel symbolized by the twelve stones of the altar on Mount Carmel. Jeremiah engaged in symbolic prophetic demonstrations such as smashing a jar and parading through the city with a yoke on his neck. Jesus' demonstration in the Temple appears to have been a symbolic enactment of its condemnation by God. The Markan framing by the cursing of the fig tree and Jesus' declaration about the (Temple) mountain being thrown into the sea indicate that in the movement Mark addresses, Jesus' demonstration was understood as God's judgment against the Temple. If Mark's account is any indication, Jesus was more specifically reenacting Jeremiah's prophetic condemnation of the Temple, accusing the incumbent high priests of being like brigands, robbing the people while using the sacrality of the Temple as their protective stronghold. Jesus' prophetic action was a direct disruptive challenge to the Roman order in Judea.

Jesus' prophetic demonstration in the Temple as portrayed in Mark also fits the dynamics of the conflict between the people and the rulers in the Israelite society of Judea and Galilee. Nowhere was the persistent conflict between rulers and ruled more dramatic than in the celebration of Passover in Jerusalem. Passover was the celebration of the liberation of the people from bondage under foreign rule of the Egyptians. Originally celebrated in families, it had been centralized in Jerusalem. But Herod had massively rebuilt the Temple in grand imperial style. And the Roman governors, to discourage any overt excitement about liberation from new foreign rule getting out of hand, habitually posted their troops atop the porticoes of the Temple courtyard to oversee the festivities. The annual celebration of exodus liberation ironically in the Temple was thus a highly charged situation. Jesus' demonstration may thus have happened under the protective disguise of Passover. Yet even though the rulers knew enough about urban mobs not to provoke them further by sending in the troops during the festivities, even a limited demonstration would have been observed, along with whatever following may have co-alesced around him.[15]

This was more than a raving "maniac" uttering mournful laments of doom over Jerusalem. Jesus of Nazareth, as a prophet who had generated a movement of renewal of Israel and sharply condemned the rulers of Is-rael, was understandably deemed a threat to the Roman imperial order. In being crucified by the Romans, however, Jesus became a martyr to the cause of the renewal of Israel under the direct rule of God. Spurred by his martyrdom in crucifixion, the movement(s) he had generated spread all the more rapidly, in Judea and Samaria as well as Galilee and beyond the frontiers of Israelite territory. Some of the results of this dynamic expan-sion of his movement(s) are the Gospels, stories produced by ordinary people, which are rare indeed in world literature.

15. On the dynamics of such an incident happening at festival time in a pre-industrial city, see Horsley, *Jesus and the Spiral of Violence*, pp. 90-99; and *Jesus and the Powers* (Minneapolis: Fortress, 2011), pp. 156-75.

Conclusion

Often cited in debates about the historical Jesus is Schweitzer's comment that scholars' interpretations of Jesus can be compared to someone looking down into a well and seeing his own image reflected. That comparison may well be pertinent to recent interpretations of Jesus as well as to the nineteenth-century interpreters that Schweitzer reviewed. Also pertinent to recent debates about Jesus is the grand claim with which Schweitzer began his *Quest of the Historical Jesus.* After predicting that German theology would stand out as a great phenomenon in modern intellectual and spiritual life, he asserted: "And the greatest achievement of German theology is the critical investigation of the life of Jesus. What it has accomplished here has laid down the conditions and determined the course of the religious thinking of the future."[1] That grandiose Christocentric, Germanocentric, and Eurocentric claim might have to be reduced to a more modest scale. Yet a hundred years later, it seems that German theology has significantly "determined the course" of investigation into the historical Jesus, and Schweitzer himself decisively influenced the debate over the "apocalyptic Jesus" that became prominent particularly in North America in the last decades.

1. Albert Schweitzer, *The Quest of the Historical Jesus* (New York: Macmillan, 1961, 1968), p. 1.

Conclusion

The study of the historical Jesus developed as a subfield of New Testament studies, which in turn developed as a branch of theological studies in modern western European culture. Those who investigate and write about Jesus are academically trained in and teach in theological schools or in university religious/theological studies departments, not in the field of history and history departments. Not surprisingly, the standard assumptions, procedures, and conceptual apparatus of historical Jesus studies have been heavily influenced or determined by modern western Christian theology. Even the understanding of history, the most basic understanding of Jesus, and the key issue to be investigated have been determined by Christian theology. History centers on the emergence of a new religion, Christianity, from another religion, Judaism. Jesus was the revealer who launched the historic transition. And the key issue is what he believed and taught. Already evident are several interrelated broad synthetic constructs according to which history and Jesus are reduced and simplified. Among these are "Judaism," "Christianity," "religion" (as separate from political-economic life), a scheme of Christian origins, and a projection of modern western individualism. The debate about the apocalyptic Jesus so prominent among American interpreters illustrates the continuing influence of the theological roots of study of the historical Jesus, both in the persistence of the synthetic construct of "apocalypticism" and in the standard focus on individual sayings.

While discussion of the historical Jesus persists in the assumptions, procedures, and concepts established up to a century ago, however, the broader field of New Testament/biblical studies has diversified into a number of subfields in the last generation, particularly in North America. A number of these subfields overlap significantly with the subject matter and sources of historical Jesus-studies. Yet the subfields proceed relatively independently of one another. In the last thirty or forty years, for example, study of the Gospels has developed an appreciation of them as whole stories. Study of late second-temple Judean texts has developed a more sophisticated understanding of apocalyptic texts, which had not received significant attention since early in the twentieth century. Studies of social-political history, including both popular and scribal movements and protests, delineated a much more precise understanding of the historical context in which Jesus worked, including the basic political-economic division and dynamics in early Roman Judea and Galilee. Given the increasing specialization of New Testament studies, however, it has evidently not been possible for those in one subfield to take into account the development in other subfields.

For study of the historical Jesus to deal with the figure who became historically significant in his historical context, three interrelated moves appear to be required. Indeed, each of these moves leads to and virtually requires taking the others.

First, developments in other subfields are calling into question some of the standard assumptions, procedures, and concepts of previous study of the historical Jesus. Interpreters of the Gospels have come to recognize them as whole stories comprised of a complex sequence of episodes with plots and subplots. To cut them up into text-fragments violates their literary integrity. More important, perhaps, is that read as sustained narratives, the Gospels present Jesus not only engaged in interaction with people in Galilee but in political-religious conflict with the high-priestly and Roman rulers in Jerusalem. Similarly, specialists on late second-temple Judean texts have come to appreciate apocalyptic texts as sustained narratives that address particular historical crises of imperial rule that conclude with an anticipated divine judgment and restoration of the people (Israel). In other areas directly relevant to investigation of the historical Jesus, recent research has shown that the Gospel stories and Jesus' speeches were orally performed and that other ancient sources, such as Josephus' histories, portray the same fundamental political-economic conflict between the rulers and the people that the Gospels do.

Second, as developments in these related areas indicate, some of the basic concepts still standard in interpretation of Jesus do not match the texts and context. They rather block recognition of particular historical circumstances, of the differences between scribal circles and the vast majority of people in village communities, of political conflicts, and of distinctive popular movements and their leaders. As laid out in Part One above, the synthetic construct of Jewish apocalypticism (centered around the "apocalyptic scenario") is a significant illustration. This concept was evidently constructed by New Testament scholars over a century ago from Gospel and Pauline text-fragments as well as verses and images taken eclectically from Jewish apocalyptic texts. But "apocalypticism" and the key events of the "apocalyptic scenario" are not attested in particular texts usually classified as apocalyptic. Nor are they attested in the (critically considered) individual sayings of Jesus. The debate about the "apocalyptic" Jesus is thus about a modern scholarly construct, not the historical texts and figures of ancient Judea and Galilee. It would help move investigation of the *historical* Jesus closer to the historical figure in the historical context, therefore, to avoid or cut through such synthetic and often essentialist scholarly constructs.

Third, again as indicated in the Gospel sources' portrayals, Jesus was engaged in interaction with people and worked in opposition to and by the rulers. Because of its focus on individual sayings and its projection of modern individualism, the recent debate about the apocalyptic Jesus, like historical Jesus study generally, constructs a Jesus who was unengaged historically. But the modern individualism of standard interpretation of Jesus can be replaced by a reconception of Jesus as a historical actor in interaction with other people in the particular circumstances and conflicts of the historical context, as outlined in Chapter 6.

These three interrelated moves necessary for investigating the *historical* Jesus in his *historical* context correspondingly involve a change in what investigators are seeking and what they may expect to find. Interpreters of Jesus believed that by focusing on individual sayings they could establish what Jesus said, the "authentic" or at least "early" words of Jesus. Jesus (or anyone else), however, could not have *communicated* by means of individual "sayings," which are later abstractions from speeches or "pronouncement" stories, etc., and hence cannot be the sources for the historical Jesus. The sources for the historical Jesus are rather the Gospels and/or their component speeches. They are representations or portrayals of Jesus comprised of Jesus traditions cultivated because they resonated with his followers. And, contrary to previous assumptions, it was the overall story in the Gospels, not the particular sayings or episodes, that were the most stable in the Gospel sources. Once we have recognized the character of our sources for Jesus, it is not possible to strive for the kind of precision on Jesus' teaching that was the goal/purpose of standard scholarship on Jesus, including both sides of the debate reviewed in Chapters 2 and 3 above. What the Gospel sources offer is a more general portrayal of key aspects of Jesus' mission and the cultural roles and patterns of social relations and meaning that he presupposed and in which he operated.

On the other hand, a relational and contextual approach as outlined above makes possible a much broader sense of Jesus in relation to people, rulers, and context, the very interactions in which history happens. Historically significant figures act in particular roles that are given in the institutional structure and/or cultural tradition of their societies. Sources for the Galilean and Judean society under Roman rule, such as the histories of Josephus, indicate that there were two principal roles, both distinctive to Israelite tradition, in which popular leaders interacted with their followers and opposed the rulers: popular messiahs/ kings and prophets who were leaders of movements of renewal and resistance. One of the earliest Gospel sources, the speeches of Q, which know nothing of Jesus as a messiah, represent Jesus throughout as speaking or acting in the role of a prophet in the revered tradition of the Israelite prophets. The other earliest source, the Gospel of Mark, knows of Jesus being understood by his closest followers as a popular king, but otherwise represents Jesus throughout in speech and action as a prophet like Moses or Elijah. Both Mark and Q, the one in narrative, the other in speeches, present Jesus' overall program as a prophet generating a movement of the renewal of Israel against the rulers of Israel.

Both of these early sources, again in different modes of presentation, represent Jesus the prophet pursuing the same key components of the renewal of Israel in interaction with the people in the crisis of viability for the fundamental social forms in which they lived, families/households and village communities. In these key aspects of his prophetic renewal program, moreover, he-and-they, interactively, build on and adapt core Israelite traditions. In his healings, the interaction of healer-healed and the people's response makes Jesus the new Elijah(-Elisha). Jesus' healings inspire further trust among the people that healing power is working through him, thus further enhancing the prophetic power/authority in Jesus-and-movement.

Other popular prophets leading movements in mid-first century Palestine called people out of their villages to experience God's new acts of deliverance. By contrast, Jesus worked directly in the village communities and their assemblies ("synagogues"). Again in a way reminiscent of Elijah's call of Elisha, Jesus commissioned protégés or envoys to expand and intensify his mission of social renewal among the village communities. As both early Gospel sources portray, in parallel but different speeches that take the traditional Mosaic covenant form, Jesus enacts in performative speech a renewal of the Mosaic covenant that had traditionally guided social-economic interaction in the village communities of Israelite society. Both the Markan covenant-renewal dialogues and the Q covenant-renewal speech indicate how Jesus' covenant renewal addressed the specific ways in which the social-economic viability of families and village communities was disintegrating under the pressures of the Roman imperial order of multiple layers of rulers and their economic demands. Jesus evidently interacted with the people in response to the most pressing problems of the historical crisis of Galilean and Judean society under Roman rule.

As portrayed in both of the earliest Gospel sources, moreover, Jesus' prophetic renewal of the people in their fundamental social forms opposed, and was opposed by, the high-priestly aristocracy based in the Temple, which was the very face of Roman imperial rule in Judea. It is clear from Josephus' histories and other Judean and Roman sources, that Roman Palestine involved a fundamental division between the vast majority of the people, on the one hand, and Roman conquerors and their client rulers, the Herodian kings and the high-priestly aristocracy, on the other. Unusual among peoples subjugated by the Romans, Judeans and Galileans persisted in protest, resistance, and periodic outright rebellion against Roman rule. All the Gospel sources — including Mark, the Q speeches, and John's Gospel — reflect this sharp divide in their representation of Jesus' prophetic speech and action.

In different forms in Mark and Q (several controversy stories and a series of prophetic woes), Jesus condemns the representatives of the Jerusalem temple-state, the scribes and Pharisees, for their role in the exploitation of the people, draining away to the Temple the economic resources needed for the mere subsistence of families. Even though the Pharisees may not have been active in Galilee itself, and certainly would not have kept Jesus under surveillance, contrary to the portrayal in Mark, the prominence of Jesus' condemnation of the scribes and Pharisees in the earliest Gospel sources must reflect a key component of his opposition to the rulers. The dominant conflict (and dominant plot) in Mark, even more emphasized in the Gospel of John, and present in some of the Q speeches, is Jesus' opposition to and by the high-priestly rulers and Temple in Jerusalem. The dominant plots of Mark and John unfold in several episodes in which Jesus pronounces or symbolically acts out God's condemnation of the Temple and/or the high priests for their oppression of the people. Not only are the forms of several of these pronouncements prophetic oracles, but in making such pronouncements and demonstrations, Jesus was acting in a traditional role of Israelite prophets such as Amos or Jeremiah, who pointedly went directly into temples to pronounce God's judgment on the rulers' exploitation of the people.

The pronouncements against the rulers, and especially the disruptive demonstration in/against the Temple, were a direct challenge to the Roman imperial order in Judea. The client high-priestly rulers and the Roman governor could hardly ignore the challenge from a leader of a movement that they probably (and reasonably) believed signaled wider resistance among the people. Indeed, Jesus' response to the Pharisees' and Herodians' attempt to entrap him over the issue of tribute to Caesar indicates precisely the kind of resistance the people in their village communities were more capable of than the handful of radical scribes and Pharisees in the Fourth Philosophy twenty-some years earlier. In the episode in Mark, Jesus declares, in a well-crafted statement, that (according to their covenant with God) the people of Israel who live directly under the rule of God do not owe and are commanded not to pay tribute to any other presumably divine ruler. The sources give no indication whatever that Jesus was somehow leading a rebellion. But his renewal of Israel was clearly in opposition to the rulers, and was threatening to the Roman imperial order. It may have appeared to the Roman governor Pontius Pilate that Jesus was another one of those popular kings leading a rebellion. Evidently Pilate crucified Jesus as a rebel leader, on the charge of having claimed to be "the king of the Judeans."

The crucified Jesus, however, thus became a martyr for the cause of his renewal of Israel under the direct rule of God. And his martyrdom motivated his followers to expand the movement(s) all the more quickly.

Moreover, his crucifixion as "king of the Judeans/Israel" may well have been one of the factors that led some of his followers to believe that after the rulers killed him he was not only vindicated by God in resurrection and exaltation to heaven, but in that exaltation was designated, in various terms, as the "Lord" and "Messiah" or "Leader and Savior" who would soon return to restore Israel (Acts 2:30, 32-36; 3:19-23; 5:30-31). For some of his followers, at least, in God's vindication of the martyred prophet who had generated the renewal of Israel was the event in which he was designated as the Messiah. Other branches of the movement he had generated, however, including those who cultivated the Q speeches and the Gospel of Mark, continued to understand Jesus only or primarily as the prophet who had launched the renewal of Israel against the rulers of Israel.

Index